Building Strategies
for GED Success

Language Arts, Reading

Steck-Vaughn

A Harcourt Achieve Imprint

www.Steck-Vaughn.com
1-800-531-5015

STAFF CREDITS

Design: Amy Braden, Deborah Diver, Joyce Spicer

Editorial: Gabrielle Field, Heera Kang, Ellen Northcutt

PHOTOGRAPHY

Page 13 ©Amy Sancetta/APWideWorld; p.19ml ©Home Services Publications, Inc.; p.19r ©Courtesy Meredith Corporation, Inc.; p.19l ©Fancy Publications, Inc.; p.19mr ©Courtesy Harris Publications, Inc.; p.29 ©Peter Andrews/APWideWorld; p.31 ©Profolio Enr./Index Stock; p.33 ©Big Cheese Photo/Alamy Images; p.45 ©Bob Daemmrich/The Image Works; p.47 ©Marianna Day Massey/CORBIS; p.48 ©Gene Herrick/APWideWorld; p.50 ©Mark Segal/Index Stock; p.52 ©Bettmann/CORBIS; p.53 ©Bettmann/CORBIS; p.65 ©Bettmann/CORBIS; p.66 ©Dan Lim/Masterfile; p.68 ©Bettmann/CORBIS; p.70 ©Stephen Frink/CORBIS; p.74 ©Reuters/CORBIS; p.79 ©Theo Allofs/CORBIS; p.86 ©Randy Lincks/Masterfile; p.90 ©Miguel Cabrera/Getty Images; p.107 ©Richard Pasley/Stock Boston; p.113 ©Rob Crandall/The Image Works; p.118 ©R.P. Kingston/Index Stock; p.121 ©Rob Crandall/The Image Works; p.122 ©Henry Ausloos/Animals Animals, Inc.; p.123 ©Mary Evans Picture Library/The Image Works; p.126 ©ColorPic/Animals Animals, Inc.

Additional photography by Photos.com; Royalty-Free/CORBIS; Royalty Free/Getty Images.

ILLUSTRATION

Rich Stergulz p.21; Franklin Ayers pp.93, 98. All other art created by Element, LLC.

ISBN 1-4190-0796-3

Contents

To the Learner

Congratulations! You have taken an important step as a lifelong learner. You have made the important decision to improve your reading skills. Read below to find out how Steck-Vaughn *Building Strategies for GED Success: Language Arts, Reading* will help you do just that.

- Take the **Pretest** on pages 3–9. Find out which skills you already know and which ones you need to practice. Mark them on the **Skills Preview Chart** on page 10.

- Study the five units in the book. Learn about nonfiction, fiction, and poetry. Check out the **GED Tips**—they've got lots of helpful information.

- Complete the **GED Skill Strategy** and **GED Test-Taking Strategy** sections. You'll learn a lot of important reading, thinking, and test-taking skills.

- As you work through the book, use the **Answers and Explanations** at the back of the book to check your own work. Study the explanations to have a greater understanding of the concepts. You can also use the **Glossary** on pages 168–169 when you want to check the meaning of a word.

- Review what you've learned by taking the **Posttest** on pages 137–144. Check the **Skills Review Chart** on page 145 to see the progress you've made!

Setting Goals

A goal is something you want to achieve. It's important to set goals in life to help you get what you want. It's also important to set goals for learning, so think carefully about what your goal is. Setting clear goals is an important part of your success. Choose your goal from those listed below. If you don't see your goal, write it on the line. You may have more than one goal.

My reading goal is to

- get my GED

- improve my daily reading skills

- increase my ability to read job-related materials

_____

A goal can take a long time to complete. To make achieving your goal easier, you can break your goal into small steps. By focusing on one step at a time, you are able to move closer and closer to achieving your goal.

Steps to your goals can include

- understanding newspaper and magazine articles

- enjoying reading stories and novels

- improving your vocabulary

- reading to your children

We hope that what you learn in this book will help you reach all of your goals.

Now take the *Reading Pretest* on pages 3–9. This will help you know what skills you need to improve so you can reach your goals.

Reading Pretest

This *Pretest* will give you an idea of the kind of work that you will be doing in this book. It will help you to figure out which reading skills you are good at and which reading skills you need to improve. You will read short passages and answer multiple-choice questions. There is no time limit.

Read each passage and question carefully. Circle the number of the correct answer.

Questions 1–3 are based on the following paragraph.

Amelia Earhart was the first female pilot to cross the Atlantic Ocean alone. Her last flight was meant to take her around the world. She and her assistant left from Florida on June 1, 1937. They made several stops along the way, including Puerto Rico, South America, and then Africa. Earhart and her assistant reached New Guinea on June 27 after completing two thirds of their trip. They left New Guinea on July 1. They were never seen again.

1. When did Earhart begin her trip around the world?

   (1) June 1, 1937
   (2) June 27, 1937
   (3) July 1, 1937
   (4) July 27, 1937

2. Which detail first hints that Earhart did not complete her last trip?

   (1) Amelia Earhart was the first female pilot.
   (2) She and her assistant began the trip on June 1.
   (3) Her last flight was meant to take her around the world.
   (4) They were never seen again.

3. According to the paragraph, where was Earhart's first stop?

   (1) Florida
   (2) Puerto Rico
   (3) Africa
   (4) New Guinea

Questions 4–7 are based on the following paragraph.

A large-scale nuclear war would result in large-scale death and destruction. Nuclear explosions would add large amounts of dust and soot to the earth's atmosphere. These clouds of ash would block out the sun in many parts of the world. The resulting cold weather would be what is called a "nuclear winter." Crops and animals would freeze, and any survivors would starve.

4. A "nuclear winter" is caused by

    (1) a cold front.
    (2) the destruction of crops and animals.
    (3) the starvation of survivors.
    (4) clouds of ash blocking the sun.

5. In the paragraph, *ash* means the same as

    (1) an explosion.
    (2) dust and soot.
    (3) sun and clouds.
    (4) the atmosphere.

6. You can conclude that a nuclear explosion would cause

    (1) temperatures to rise.
    (2) the sun to freeze.
    (3) temperatures to lower.
    (4) no effect on temperatures.

crop vt. (kräp) 1. to cut the tops off—**n.** (kräp) 1. a group 2. a body part in earthworms and some insects 3. a food product grown on a farm

7. Look to the left at the different meanings for *crop* found in a dictionary. Which meaning for *crop* is used in the paragraph?

    (1) to cut the tops off
    (2) a group
    (3) a body part in earthworms and some insects
    (4) a food product grown on a farm

Questions 8–11 are based on the following letter to the editor.

To the Editor:

Our mayor, Gale Smith, was elected over three years ago. Smith promised to clean up city government, but she hasn't. She said that she would get rid of dishonest officials. But not one person has been fired, even though there is proof that five officials have broken the law. They have taken bribes and mishandled our city's funds. The mayor has let us all down. Is she a crook, too? Think about this when you vote next month!

8. What is the main idea of the letter?

    (1) Five city officials have not been fired.

    (2) City funds have been mishandled.

    (3) The mayor has failed to keep her promise.

    (4) The mayor has been in office more than three years.

9. According to the letter, five city officials broke the law when they

    (1) took bribes.

    (2) mishandled the election.

    (3) failed to fire dishonest officials.

    (4) promised to clean up city government.

10. Which statement expresses an opinion?

    (1) Smith promised to clean up city government.

    (2) The mayor has let us all down.

    (3) Smith was elected over three years ago.

    (4) Not one person has been fired.

11. Which detail tells you that Smith is running for mayor again?

    (1) Our mayor, Gale Smith, was elected over three years ago.

    (2) She said she would get rid of dishonest officials.

    (3) Think about this when you vote next month!

    (4) both (1) and (2)

Questions 12–14 are based on the following letter.

Dear Mr. Stuart,

This notice is to inform you of a change in your health insurance payment. Our records show that you turned 50 last month. As a result, your rate has increased. Your new payment amount is shown on the attached page.

Your health insurance rate is based on your age, where you live, and what type of work you do. We review everyone's policy on certain birthdays. These reviews take place when policy holders turn 25, 30, 35, 40, 45, 50, 55, 60, and 65.

If you have questions, please call Customer Service at 1-800-555-2305.

Sincerely,
Member Services

12. The letter tells mostly about
    (1) a change in a man's health insurance rate.
    (2) the many ways insurance rates are determined.
    (3) the different times insurance rates are reviewed.
    (4) a man who recently had a birthday.

13. An insurance policy is reviewed when a policy holder
    (1) moves to a new city.
    (2) changes job.
    (3) turns a certain age.
    (4) all of the above

14. You can infer that Mr. Stuart's last review was
    (1) ten years ago.
    (2) five years ago.
    (3) when he was 40.
    (4) when he was 55.

Questions 15–17 are based on the following movie review.

Ray is a must-see film about the life of beloved musician Ray Charles. Many movies about famous people glorify their subject. Ray, however, presents a story about a man who is a brilliant musician but a flawed human being. Actor Jamie Foxx serves up yet another inspired performance as the beloved Charles—capturing his walk, talk, and style. Foxx's incredible performance and the story of Ray Charles' life make Ray a film you won't soon forget.

15. What describes the reviewer's reaction to Foxx's performance?

    (1) enthusiastic
    (2) bored
    (3) disappointed
    (4) unimpressed

16. According to the reviewer, how is Ray different from most movies about famous people?

    (1) It just shows the good side of Charles's life.
    (2) It shows both sides of Charles's character.
    (3) It stars Jamie Foxx.
    (4) It is a movie that is not easy to forget.

17. According to the reviewer, how is this similar to Foxx's other performances?

    (1) He plays the role of a musician.
    (2) He is brilliant.
    (3) He has the leading role.
    (4) He plays the role of a real person.

Some boys are very tough. They're afraid of nothing. They are the ones who climb a wall and take a bow at the top. Not only are they brave on the roof, but they make a lot of noise in the darkest part of the cellar where even the super hates to go. They also jiggle and hop on the platform between the locked doors of the subway cars.

Four boys are jiggling on the swaying platform. Their names are Alfred, Calvin, Samuel, and Tom. The men and the women in the cars on either side watch them. They don't like them to jiggle or jump but don't want to interfere. Of course some of the men in the cars were once brave boys like these. One of them had ridden the tail of a speeding truck from New York to Rockaway Beach without getting off, without his sore fingers losing hold. Nothing happened to him then or later. He had made a compact with other boys who preferred to watch: Starting at Eighth Avenue and Fifteenth Street, he would get to some specified place, maybe Twenty-third and the river, by hopping the tops of moving trucks. This was hard to do when one truck turned a corner in the wrong direction and the nearest truck was a couple of feet too high. He made three or four starts before succeeding. He had gotten this idea from a film at school called *The Romance of Logging*. He had finished high school, married a good friend, was in a responsible job and going to night school.

From "Samuel" by Grace Paley,
Enormous Changes at the Last Minute

18. Where does the story take place?

(1) on the roof of an apartment building

(2) in the cellar of an apartment building

(3) on the subway

(4) at Rockaway Beach

19. As the passage continues, it will likely tell more about

(1) the many ways in which tough boys behave.

(2) the man on the train who once hopped on moving trucks.

(3) the passengers who don't want the boys to jiggle on the platform.

(4) the different stops the subway car will make.

Questions 20–21 are based on the following poem.

LOST

Desolate[1] and lone

All night long on the lake

Where fog trails and mist creeps,

The whistle of a boat

Calls and cries unendingly,

Like some lost child

In tears and trouble

Hunting the harbor's breast

And the harbor's eyes.

[1]isolated, unhappy   Carl Sandburg, *Chicago Poems* ©1916

20. What is the mood of the poem?

(1) bitter

(2) hopeful

(3) angry

(4) lonely

21. The boat's whistle is compared to a lost child to help create

(1) a helpless and abandoned feeling.

(2) a picture of the mist and fog on a dark night.

(3) a desire to help children who are lost.

(4) an image of the lake and harbor.

When you finish the *Reading Pretest*, check your answers on page 148. Then look at the chart on page 10.

Skills Preview Chart

This chart shows you which skills you need to study. Check your answers. In the first column, circle the number of any questions you missed. Then look across the row to find out which skills you should review as well as the page numbers on which you can find the instruction on those skills.

Questions	Skill	Pages
1	Scanning	12–17
2	Predicting	18–23
5	Using Context Clues	24–31
7	Understanding Multiple Meanings	32–35
8	Finding the Stated Main Idea	44–49
12	Determining the Implied Main Idea	50–53
11, 13	Locating Supporting Details	54–57
3	Showing Time Order	66–69
16, 17	Comparing and Contrasting	70–73
4	Showing Cause and Effect	74–77
9	Giving Examples	78–81
14	Making Inferences	90–93
6	Drawing Conclusions	94–97
10	Identifying Fact and Opinion	98–101
15	Detecting Bias	102–105
18	Understanding Character and Setting	114–117
19	Understanding Plot and Conflict	118–121
20	Understanding Theme and Mood	122–125
21	Understanding Imagery in Poetry	126–129

Unit 1 Reading for Meaning

chapter

scan

context

article

In this unit you will learn about

- scanning
- predicting
- using context to find meaning
- understanding multiple meanings of words

When you pick up a book or magazine, do you flip through it? If you look at the titles, headings, and pictures before you read, you are previewing. You are getting an idea of what is inside the book or magazine.

Preview the title, vocabulary words, and pictures in Lesson 1. What do you think the lesson is about?

_____

_____

When you read, you may come across words that you don't know. Think about what you do when this happens.

Later in this unit, you will read the word *bibliophile*. What will you do when you see this word?

_____

_____

specific
particular; a certain kind

passage
a short piece of writing that is several paragraphs long

paragraph
a group of one or more sentences about one idea or topic

scanning
quickly running your eyes over a passage to look for specific information

Sometimes when you read, you are looking for **specific** information. You may not have time to read a whole article, chapter, or **passage**. You may want to find the information you are looking for quickly. Let's say you want to know today's weather. You check the newspaper. You look for the headline, chart, or **paragraph** that seems like it may have the information you want to know. Looking for specific information is called **scanning**.

Suppose you are looking for an apartment. You don't want to spend more than $950 a month. Therefore, the only ads you need to read are those for apartments renting for $950 per month or less. You can ignore the others.

Scan these ads from a newspaper. Place a check (✓) next to the ads for apartments that rent for $950 or less. Run your eyes over the ads and look for dollar amounts. Scan each ad just for the information you need.

ELEGANT 1 bedrm., very bright, nice view. New ktchn., dishwshr., carpet, and curtains incl. No pets. $1100. 555-9902

BIG 1 Bedrm. in excel. condition. Furnished, queen bed, new carpet, tile bth., new stove. No fee. $950. 555-5004

NEWLY RENOV. 2 bedrm., balcony, washer/dryer, lg. ktchn., dishwshr., near bus. No pets. $1250. 555-9095

BRIGHT, 2 bedrm. top flr. of house. Big bath. Heat incl. No pets. $930. 555-1413

WOMAN seeks rmmate. Own bedrm. in 2 bedrm. apt. No smoker or pet. $550. 555-2209

Check your answers on page 150.

The following passage is about golfer Tiger Woods. Suppose you want to find out his score on Saturday at the Masters Tournament.

Scan the passage to find Tiger's score on Saturday.

The Masters lasts for four days. Golfers play one round each day. They begin on Thursday. Tiger began the first round poorly. He shot a score of 40 on the first nine holes. That score was four over par. Tiger knew that he had to play better in order to win. Tiger shot six under par on the next nine holes. His score for the day was 70. He was in fourth place.

Tiger's scores improved as the tournament continued. Friday, he had a score of 66. Saturday, he shot a 65. Those scores were among the best in the tournament's history. Tiger was in control. He was nine strokes ahead of the second-place golfer. Only one day remained in the tournament.

Tiger did not disappoint his fans on Sunday. The record tournament score at the Masters was 271. Tiger could tie the record with a score of 70 for Sunday's round. Instead, Tiger shot a 69 to break the record. His final score was 270.

From *Tiger Woods* by Elizabeth Sirimarco

Write down Tiger's score on Saturday. _____

Were you able to quickly find the information you needed? Here is one way you could have quickly found Tiger's score for Saturday. You are looking for information about a specific day of the week. You know that the days of the week are **capitalized**. Look through the passage for words that begin with a capital letter. In the second paragraph, you see the words *Friday* and *Saturday*. Tiger's score for Saturday is given there. His score was 65.

capitalize
to begin a word with a capital letter

Some kinds of information are easier to find than others. For example, because **proper names** are capitalized, they stand out in a passage and are easy to find. They name a particular person (*George Washington*), place (*Chicago*), or thing (*the Statue of Liberty*).

Numbers also stand out in a passage. Looking for numbers can help you find a score, a telephone number, or an address. You can find a telephone number by looking for a seven-digit or ten-digit string of numbers. To find addresses, look for numbers as well as capital letters for street and city names.

Dates are easy to find as well. Sometimes a date is written like this–June 14, 2005–with the name of a month, which is a proper noun and therefore capitalized, and a number. Other times, a date is written with just numbers (6/14/05).

Read the following questions. Try to find the answers in the newspaper article below <u>without</u> reading the whole passage.

1. What is the fee for a dog license?

_____

2. When is the deadline for getting a pet license?

_____

> ### Renew Pet Licenses
>
> The Board of Health is reminding residents that it's time to renew licenses for pets. All cats and dogs must be licensed. The deadline is January 15. The fee for cats is $10.00 per year. The fee for dogs is $15.00 per year. You may renew your pet's license at City Hall between 9:00 A.M. and 4:30 P.M., Monday through Friday.

Check your answers on page 150.

Sometimes a test question tells you what kind of information you need to find in a passage.

Read the test question. Then scan the passage below for the answer. Circle the number of the correct answer.

How does the special clothing that nurses and doctors wear protect them?

(1) It keeps them from being cut by sharp scalpels.

(2) It protects their eyes from chemicals.

(3) It protects them and their patients from germs.

(4) It identifies them as being doctors and nurses.

> Many jobs require the use of special clothing. Some special clothing can identify the worker. For example, you can identify a police officer because of the uniform he or she wears. Other work clothing is for protection. A construction worker wears a hard hat for protection from accidents on the job. Nurses and doctors usually wear clothing that has been sterilized. This protects them and their patients from germs.

To find the answer in the paragraph above, what kind of information did you look for? You wanted to know about the clothing nurses and doctors wear, so you scanned the passage for the words *clothing, nurses,* and *doctors*.

Once you found the words you wanted, you read the sentence where those words were found. The information you found matched one of the answers.

Tests often have reading passages followed by several questions. There may be words in a passage that you don't know. You may be able to answer the questions anyway, even if you don't understand every word in the passage. For example, in the paragraph above about special clothing, you could answer the question even if you didn't understand the words *accidents* or *sterilized*.

GED Tip

Scanning can save you time on the GED Reading Test. To quickly find an answer, scan the passage for key words or numbers that may give you the information you need.

Check your answer on page 150.

Questions 1–4 are based on the product label shown on the right. The label is from a can of cleaning spray.

Write the answer below.

1. Read the label. Suppose you don't like something about the product. Where would you send a letter to complain?

   _____

   _____

   _____

Circle the number of the correct answer.

2. When you were looking for information to answer question 1, you knew you had to find

   (1) a telephone number.
   (2) a person's name.
   (3) the name of a business.
   (4) the name of a business and an address.

3. Suppose your friend just got some spray in her eyes. You want to know what to do. You would read the part of the label that begins with the word or words

   (1) Flammable.
   (2) First Aid.
   (3) Warning.
   (4) To clean.

4. Suppose that you have never used this spray before. You want to know how long to spray a surface. Which word or words would you look for?

   (1) Flammable
   (2) First Aid
   (3) To clean
   (4) Do not use

Warning: Avoid contact with food. Avoid spraying into eyes.

Flammable! Contents are under pressure. Do not use near flame or fire. Do not puncture or incinerate container.

First Aid: If sprayed into eyes, immediately flush with plenty of cool water. Get medical attention if irritation continues.

To clean:
1. Hold can upright 8" to 10" from surface.
2. Spray surface 2 to 3 seconds until covered.
Do not use on wood furniture or acrylic plastics.

Lavalle Household Products
293 Bloomfield Ave.
Montclair, NJ 07043

Made in USA

Questions 5–7 are based on the following paragraph.

Many famous people have had disabilities. They have been blind or deaf or have lost the use of one or more limbs. The famous composer Ludwig van Beethoven lost most of his hearing by age 32. He was completely deaf at age 46. Still, he kept writing music. He also led orchestras even though he could not hear the music they played. French actress Sarah Bernhardt lost her leg after an accident in 1914. Yet she performed on stage until her death in 1923. Helen Keller was both blind and deaf from the age of two. When grown, she became a skilled speaker and wrote ten books. Franklin D. Roosevelt had his legs paralyzed from polio. He became president in 1933. Henri de Toulouse-Lautrec had a bad fall when he was 14. He damaged both of his legs, which limited his growth. He went on to become a famous French painter.

Circle the number of the correct answer.

5. Which person had more than one disability?

    (1) Ludwig van Beethoven

    (2) Henri de Toulouse-Lautrec

    (3) Franklin D. Roosevelt

    (4) Helen Keller

6. What happened in 1914?

    (1) Franklin D. Roosevelt became president.

    (2) Sarah Bernhardt lost her leg.

    (3) Helen Keller became blind and deaf.

    (4) Henri de Toulouse–Lautrec had a bad fall.

7. What was the cause of Franklin D. Roosevelt's disability?

    (1) He fell.

    (2) He had a car accident.

    (3) He had polio.

    (4) both (1) and (2)

Check your answers on page 150.

predict
to use information you know to guess what will happen later

You **predict** things every day. Imagine one evening you look out the window and see snow falling. A little later the weather reporter on TV says that it's going to snow all night and that the temperature will stay in the teens. You can predict, or guess, that the roads will be icy and dangerous the next morning. Being able to use this information to predict what will happen is helpful. If you have to drive to work or school, you know you will need to leave earlier than usual. Traffic is often heavy and slow when roads are icy and dangerous. Also, if your car doesn't have snow tires, you have time to find some other, safer way to get to work or school.

Here is another way that predicting can be helpful. Imagine you want to take a friend to a movie. You open the newspaper and you see this movie ad.

DAY STAR PICTURES PRESENTS A SIMON COBB PRODUCTION SPACE COLONY.
STARRING CHLOE ERHARDT ISAAC BROCKMAN MARITA HANNA MASON HOWARD ELI FOLEY WILLIAM RICHARDS
LAUREN AMPARO AND SOFIE MCALLISTER SCREENPLAY BY ZOE AND MALCOLM WASHINGTON PRODUCED BY MAXINE DISOTO
ROGER MATHERS AND DANA SIRROW DIRECTED BY TOBIAS BLUTH COSTUME DESIGNER TRACI RADCLIFF PRODUCTION DESIGN DONNA WALSTOUT

Is this a romantic movie? A comedy? A children's movie? Based on the information on the poster, it isn't hard to figure out that this is a science fiction movie. If your friend likes science fiction, you can predict that this may be a movie he or she would like.

Predicting can help you when you read, too. Suppose you want to begin a project. You want to find specific information about how to build a wooden planter. How will you decide which of the four magazines below will help you? Scan the pictures and words on the covers of each magazine to learn what's inside.

The Family Handyman most likely has the information you need.

Now look at the **table of contents** for *The Family Handyman* below. The table of contents lists the **articles** found in the magazine.

Underline the title of the article about planters.

Table of Contents

You should have underlined "Easy-to-Make Planters," found on page 38. Now let's say you want to add a design to your planter to make it look like a basket. To find out if this kind of planter is described in the article, preview the article to get an idea of what it is about. Then you can predict if the article will be helpful to you.

table of contents
a listing of the articles found in a magazine or a listing of the parts of a book

article
a complete piece of writing in a magazine or newspaper

To preview an article, look at the first few sentences. Read the first two sentences from "Easy-to-Make Planters."

> **Building a planter** for your flowers starts with a simple plywood box. Once you make the box, we'll show you how to add your own design touches to make the planter you want.

These first two sentences tell you that almost any type of planter can be made from a simple box. It's up to the builder to give it a special look. This article seems to have the information you need.

Suppose you're looking for information in a book. The table of contents usually gives you an idea of the information found in each **chapter**. If the table of contents is not helpful, the first few sentences of a chapter often tell you what the chapter is about.

Here is another table of contents. This one is from a book called *Getting to Know Computers*.

chapter
the parts that a book is divided into

Table of Contents

Use the table of contents above to answer the questions.

1. What do you think Chapter 4 is about?

    _____

2. Which chapter is about how computers work?

    _____

Check your answers on page 150.

You probably predicted that Chapter 3 is about how computers work. Perhaps you knew that *mechanics* means "the way something works." Perhaps when you looked at the other titles, none of them seemed to fit what you wanted to know. However you chose the answer, you made a guess based on what you know.

Most of the chapter titles in *Getting to Know Computers* give you an idea of what kind of information you can find in the chapter. Look at the title of Chapter 6 on page 20. It may not be clear from this title what the chapter is about. However, if you turn to the first page of the chapter and read a few sentences, you will probably be able to guess what it is about. Read the beginning of Chapter 6 below.

GED Tip

You may have to go back to the passage to answer a question on the GED Reading Test. Read the first few sentences of each paragraph and predict whether the information you need is in that paragraph.

Chapter 6 Around the World in 80 Seconds

Imagine being able to talk to anyone, anywhere in the world, anytime. That's what the Internet can do. With just a few pieces of equipment, you can be connected to anyone in the world in about a minute. You can get the news, the weather, and the latest in sports, and entertainment. The Internet brings the world to you.

You may have predicted that this chapter is about communicating using the computer. By looking at the picture, you can also predict that the chapter will describe how you can talk to people around the world using a computer and a telephone. You have made an **educated guess**, or a prediction, about what kind of information the chapter contains.

educated guess
a guess you make based on what you already know

Circle the number of the correct answer.

1. You want to coach your daughter's soccer team. Which
    of these books contains the information you need?

    (1) *The History of Track and Field Sports*
    (2) *The Official Guidebook of Soccer Rules*
    (3) *Famous Soccer Players from Around the World*
    (4) *Pelé: The King of Soccer*

2. You want to know what to do if you burn yourself with boiling water.
    Which of these books would be most helpful?

    (1) *Home Accidents—What to Do in an Emergency*
    (2) *Safety Tips from the American Health Association*
    (3) *Injuries on the Playing Field*
    (4) both (1) and (2)

3. You are interested in new laws about tenants and landlords. Which
    of these newspaper articles should you read?

    (1) Gonzalez Plans Five New Apartment Buildings
    (2) Very Few Empty Apartments Left in the City
    (3) Landlords Against New Rent-Control Laws
    (4) Looking for a Good Place to Live

4. Which of the articles listed in question 3 should you read if you want
    to move to a new apartment?

    (1) Articles 1 and 2
    (2) Articles 2 and 3
    (3) Article 2
    (4) Article 4

Read the tables of contents from the two books below. Then complete the chart at the bottom of the page. Fill in the number of the book and the name of the chapter where you would find the information.

Book 1

TAKING CARE OF YOUR HOME

Book 2

YOU AND THE LAW

Information Needed	Book	Chapter
what to do if you want to sell your car	2	You and Your Property
what to do if the sink drain is clogged		
what to do if all the lights go out		
what to do if you are renting an apartment and get an eviction notice		

Check your answers on page 150.

When you read, you will sometimes find words you don't understand. How do you find out what the words mean? If a word is alone without any other words around it, you may have a hard time figuring out its meaning. For example, you may not know what this word means:

aquarium

Is it a person, place, or thing? Does it describe a person, place, or thing? There is no easy way to figure out what a word means when it is not used in a sentence. When you read the word in **context**, though, you may be able to figure out its meaning. The words and sentences near an unfamiliar word are the word's context. They can help you figure out what the word means.

context
the words and sentences that help you figure out the meaning of an unfamiliar word

Read the paragraph and answer the question below.

Starting Your Own Aquarium

You can make an interesting aquarium for very little money. First, put some clean sand or stones in the bottom of a glass tank. Then, get some water plants from a pet store and push them into the sand. Next, fill the tank with water. Wait about a day until the water has cleared. Now you are ready to add some small fish. Sit back and enjoy your new aquarium.

What do you think the word *aquarium* means?

_____

_____

Look at the context for the word *aquarium*. The paragraph contains many clues about the word's meaning. An aquarium is a glass tank. It is a place where fish live. An aquarium is filled with water. It has plants and sand or stones. From the word's context, you can make an educated guess about its meaning.

Read the paragraph and answer the question below.

We had a wonderful day at the zoo. After looking at the monkeys, we decided to find the birds. We saw a big sign that said AVIARY, so we headed in that direction. When we got to the aviary, I was amazed. The building was huge, and there were hundreds of different birds inside. The birds were every color of the rainbow.

What do you think the word *aviary* means?

_____

_____

You may not know the meaning of the word *aviary*. You may not know what it is made of or exactly how it looks. But the word's context describes a place full of birds, so an aviary must be a place where birds are kept.

You can figure out the meaning of a word from the word's context, because the words and sentences near an unfamiliar word often give clues to the word's meaning. Sometimes, a passage even contains the **definition**, or meaning, of a word.

definition
an explanation of a word's meaning

Read the paragraph and answer the questions on the next page.

Raccoons thrive because they are adaptable—they are able to change their behavior to suit their situation. They will eat almost anything. With their nimble front paws—and a great deal of curiosity—raccoons can find whatever food is available, according to the season. Raccoons have a keen sense of touch. They are always poking their fingers into crevices, searching for small animals, such as mice and insects, to eat. They can even open garbage cans and live well on the contents. Near farms, they help themselves to fruit, vegetables, and grain.

From *Mammals: A Multimedia Encyclopedia* by the National Geographic Society

A raccoon

1. What do you think *adaptable* means?

_____

_____

2. What clue in the passage helped you figure out the word's meaning?

_____

_____

punctuation

marks that make sentences easier to understand. Periods, commas, dashes, and colons are examples of punctuation.

Punctuation can give you clues to a word's meaning in a passage. A dash (—) or a comma (,) is often a clue that more information about a word will follow. Look at the dash on page 25 in the first sentence of the paragraph about raccoons. The meaning of *adaptable* follows the dash.

Read the paragraph. Underline the sentence that includes a word and its definition. Then answer the questions.

When you write, you usually don't want to use the same words over and over again. To avoid repeating a word, you might use a synonym, or a word that has the same or almost the same meaning as another word. For example, a synonym for *pretty* is *attractive*. A dictionary often includes synonyms after a word's definition.

3. What word was defined in the sentence you underlined?

_____

4. What is the meaning of the word that was defined?

_____

_____

5. What punctuation gave you a clue that a word was being defined?

_____

Check your answers on page 151.

Sometimes writers use punctuation to set off a list of examples that give clues to a word's meaning.

Read the ad on the right. Then answer the questions.

1. What does *apparel* mean?

_____

2. What examples give you a clue to the word's meaning?

_____

Another way writers set off a list or a definition is by using a colon (:). Writers may also set off the definition of a word by using *like*, *such as*, or *for example*.

Read the example below.

Many fire departments count on their auxiliary: people who offer to help in whatever way they can during a fire. The auxiliary is not a part of the regular team that fights the fire, yet they help in many ways. Some people call them the unsung heroes of the fire department.

Firefighters battling a fire

Can you figure out what *auxiliary* means? Look at the words that follow the colon. If you think that *auxiliary* means people who offer to help during a fire, you are correct.

Check your answers on page 151.

A writer does not always use an example to tell you what a word means. Sometimes you can guess what a word means because you are told what it doesn't mean. Words like *but*, *while*, *on the other hand*, *although*, and *however* tell you that two things are different, or opposites.

Read the paragraph. Try to figure out what *extrovert* means.

> George and Jen are brother and sister, but they are quite different. Jen is shy and likes to spend time by herself. George, on the other hand, is a real extrovert. Jen prefers to play quietly, while George is often boisterous when he plays. Jen is also very neat. George, however, throws his clothes and toys all over the place. Sometimes it looks like a hurricane came through his room!

The paragraph says that Jen is shy and likes to be by herself. The words *on the other hand* in the third sentence are a clue that George is very different. He is an *extrovert*. The word *extrovert* must mean the opposite of *shy*—an extrovert is someone who is outgoing and likes to be with other people.

Read the questions below and write your answers.

1. What does *boisterous* mean?

_____

2. What word gives a clue to the meaning of *boisterous*?

_____

3. The word *unkempt* describes someone who looks sloppy. Write a sentence using the word *unkempt* and a clue (comma, dash, an example or opposite) that tells what *unkempt* means.

_____

_____

Check your answers on page 151.

GED Tip

When taking the GED Reading Test, use clues in a passage to help you understand unfamiliar words. Look for punctuation, examples, and other clues to figure out a word's meaning.

Questions 1–8 are based on the following paragraph.

Away from his village, however, Nelson [Mandela] came face-to-face with the way blacks were treated by the whites who ruled South Africa. At his college, black students had a lot of say in how their school was run. But while he was there, the white authorities decided to take much of that power away. Nelson tried to stop this by organizing a *protest*. A protest happens when a group of people get together to fight against something they believe is unfair. In this case, Nelson helped convince his fellow students not to go to class until the school agreed to give them back the rights they had lost. Instead of winning back the students' rights, however, Nelson was suspended from school and had to return home.

From *Nelson Mandela* by Brian Feinberg

Nelson Mandela

Circle the number of the correct answer.

1. A *protest* is
   (1) a group of college students.
   (2) South African authorities.
   (3) a group of people who get together to fight something they think is unfair.
   (4) a school in South Africa.

2. The word *suspended* means
   (1) won rights.
   (2) sent away.
   (3) voted.
   (4) traveled.

3. The words that give a clue to the meaning of *suspended* are

    (1) "people get together."

    (2) "and had to return home."

    (3) "winning the students' rights."

    (4) "his fellow students."

4. The word *authorities* means people

    (1) in power.

    (2) who vote.

    (3) who teach.

    (4) who go to school.

5. The word *college* means

    (1) community.

    (2) family.

    (3) school.

    (4) classroom.

6. The words that give a clue to the meaning of *college* are

    (1) "ruled" and "a lot of say."

    (2) "group of people" and "unfair."

    (3) "winning" and "rights."

    (4) "students" and "their school."

7. The word *convince* means

    (1) discuss.

    (2) forget.

    (3) talk into.

    (4) leave.

8. The word *fellow* means

    (1) a person who fights.

    (2) a person in the same group.

    (3) a voter.

    (4) a villager.

The Mississippi River is great at building land. When the river floods, it carries rich deposits of mud and sand to its lower shores. These deposits create fertile farmland. The Mississippi River also carries deposits to the Gulf of Mexico. Over time, these deposits have settled and become sediment. The sediment has formed a delta… a low plain of land found at the mouth of the river. A delta is shaped much like a triangle. The name *delta* comes from the fourth letter of the Greek alphabet. Like the land, this capital letter is also shaped like a triangle.

The Mississippi River

Circle the number of the correct answer.

9. The word *deposits* means

   (1) parts of the Mississippi River.
   (2) mud and sand that the river carries to different places along the river.
   (3) water, mud, and sand that is mixed and used as building material.
   (4) kinds of farms.

10. In the third sentence, *fertile* means

    (1) good for making building material.
    (2) carried away by floods.
    (3) near the Mississippi River.
    (4) good for growing things.

11. In the fifth sentence, *sediment* means

    (1) deposits that settle at the bottom of a body of water.
    (2) an area of land along the shores of a river.
    (3) the mouth of a river.
    (4) a three-sided shape.

12. In the sixth sentence, *delta* means

    (1) the fourth letter of the Greek alphabet.
    (2) a land deposit at the mouth of a river.
    (3) an area of land along the shores of a river.
    (4) good farmland.

Check your answers on page 151.

When you read, you may come across a word that you know but that doesn't make sense in the passage. The word has more than one meaning. When you look up the word in the dictionary, you see a list of meanings. Look for the meaning that makes sense in the context of the passage.

Read the paragraph and dictionary definitions.

> What is the key to Steven Spielberg's success? He has great talent. He works hard. (Sometimes he works twenty-four hours a day!) But perhaps the real key to Steven's success is that he remembers who his audience is. Steven never forgets that he is making his movies for a kid sitting in a dark theater—a kid filled with excitement, waiting for the magic to begin.
>
> From *Meet Steven Spielberg* by Thomas Conklin

[1]**key** (kē) *n.* a metal instrument used to unlock a door

[2]**key** *n.* a word, phrase, or idea that explains why or how something happens

[3]**key** *n.* a low island or reef

[1]**kid** (kĭd) *n.* a young person, a child

[2]**kid** *n.* a young goat

[3]**kid** *v.* to joke with or have fun with

Use the definitions to answer these questions.

1. Write the meaning of *key* that fits best in the paragraph.

_____

_____

2. Write the meaning of *kid* that fits best in the paragraph.

_____

_____

Check your answers on page 152.

GED Tip

When taking the GED Reading Test, if a word that you know doesn't make sense, look at its context. Use the context to figure out a different meaning for the word.

Read the following paragraphs. Use the dictionary definitions on page 32 to answer the questions.

1. This was Keesha's big day. She had passed her driving test at last. Today she was going to use the car for the first time. As she pulled on her coat, she reached into the pocket. Suddenly her heart jumped. The key! It was gone!

   Which meaning of *key* best fits in this paragraph?

   _____

   _____

2. The kids butted their heads together playfully. Their mother paid no attention as she grazed in the field nearby.

   Which meaning of *kid* best fits in this paragraph?

   _____

   _____

3. As brothers, James and Ricardo could not be more different. James is very serious, but Ricardo likes to kid around most of the time. Both boys are good students.

   Which meaning of *kid* best fits in this paragraph?

   _____

   _____

Check your answers on page 152.

Questions 1–3 are based on the following paragraph.

> My mother did not like the thought of my being an actress and told me I would probably faint under the bright lights. She also did not like the idea of my being a tap dancer, so I was never allowed to take lessons. Missionaries, as everyone knew, were sometimes eaten alive, so that left teaching and opera singing. Writing, which was the thing I loved most in the world, was only my hobby.
>
> From *How I Came to Be A Writer*
> by Phyllis Reynolds Naylor

Circle the number of the correct answer.

1. What does *faint* mean in this paragraph?

    (1) dim
    (2) lacking courage
    (3) weak
    (4) to fall down and lose consciousness

2. What does *tap* mean in this paragraph?

    (1) a kind of dance
    (2) a faucet that brings water
    (3) to strike lightly
    (4) to select or choose

3. What does *left* mean in this paragraph?

    (1) the side that is not the right side
    (2) what remained
    (3) a certain political view
    (4) a direction

Questions 4–7 are based on the following passage.

As he stands in the grocery store, Kham checks his list—
a bag of oranges, bananas, bread, tuna, milk, and a pound of coffee.
He likes to cross each item off as he puts it in his cart.

The last thing Kham decides to get is some cherries. As he is
checking out, he places his bag of cherries on the scale. Suddenly,
the bag breaks—there are cherries all over the floor! The cherries
are ruined, so Kham has to go back to the produce section
for more.

Circle the number of the correct answer.

4. What does *pound* mean in this passage?

   (1) to hit hard
   (2) a unit of measurement
   (3) a place to keep stray animals
   (4) a bag

5. What does *scale* mean in this passage?

   (1) to climb
   (2) a range of musical notes
   (3) a machine used to weigh things
   (4) part of the skin of a fish

6. What does *cross* mean in this passage?

   (1) upset
   (2) the intersection of two pieces
   (3) to strike out or remove
   (4) to pass over, as on a bridge

7. What does *produce* mean in this passage?

   (1) to make something
   (2) to present a movie or TV show
   (3) fruits and vegetables
   (4) the amount that is made

Check your answers on page 152.

GED Skill Strategy

Figuring Out Word Meaning

Context clues can help you to understand new words when you read. Context clues are the words and sentences around an unfamiliar word. Punctuation may also be a clue.

> ▶ **Strategy** Read the paragraph. Ask yourself: What clues will I use to help me understand the meaning of an unfamiliar word?
>
> 1. Think about the unfamiliar word's context. What is the sentence or paragraph about?
>
> 2. Look for clues in punctuation. Commas and dashes can set off a clue to a word's meaning.
>
> 3. Look for key words. Some key words are *such as, like,* and *for example*.

Exercise 1: Read the paragraph. Then answer the questions. Circle the letter of the correct answer.

Library to Build New Wing

Local philanthropist Brit Fox said today that she will donate money to build a new wing at the library. Ms. Fox said that those with wealth should give freely to help their communities. Thanks to Ms. Fox, the bibliophiles of Hillsboro will have more space next year. They can enjoy their beloved books in the library's new wing.

1. What does *philanthropist* mean?

   (a) someone who likes libraries
   (b) someone who gives money to worthy projects

2. What does *bibliophile* mean?

   (a) book lover
   (b) librarian

Many words have more than one meaning. These words are called multiple-meaning words. When you look up a word in the dictionary, you may find it has several definitions. Use the word's context to decide which definition fits best in a passage.

> ▶ **Strategy** Read the paragraph. Ask yourself: If a word doesn't make sense, does it have another meaning? If I look in the dictionary, can I figure out the correct meaning of the word from the context?
>
> 1. Look up the word in a dictionary. Read each definition.
>
> 2. Choose the definition that fits the context of the word.
>
> 3. Check your choice. Read the sentence again with the definition in place of the word.

Exercise 2: Read each paragraph and answer the questions.

The steel workers were angry about how things were run at the plant. Their pay was too low. Their work was too dangerous. They voted to go on strike to force the owner of the plant to make changes.

> ¹**strike** (strīk) *v.* to hit something
>
> ²**strike** *v.* to cancel something out
>
> ³**strike** *n.* a work stoppage by employees

3. Look in the margin at the dictionary meanings for *strike*. Which meaning fits best in the paragraph? Write the definition and tell why it fits.

_____

_____

Everyone in the theater enjoyed the play so much they stood up and cheered at the end. The play was a huge hit.

> ¹**hit** (hĭt) *v.* to strike a blow
>
> ²**hit** *n.* a big success
>
> ³**hit** *v.* in baseball, to strike a ball with the bat

4. Look in the margin at the dictionary meanings for *hit*. Which meaning fits best in the paragraph? Write the definition and tell why it fits.

_____

_____

Check your answers on page 152.

Previewing Test Questions

On the GED Reading Test, you answer questions based on reading passages.

One strategy for passing the GED Test is to preview the questions before reading the passage. This will help you know what to look for as you read.

 Strategy   Try this strategy with the following example. Use these steps.

Step 1   Read the question. What is it asking you to find out?

Step 2   Read the passage. Look for what the question asked you to find out.

Step 3   Answer the question.

WHY DID LINCOLN'S LIFE CHANGE?

Abe Lincoln was a poor boy. He was born in 1809 and raised on the frontier in Kentucky and Indiana. Living on the frontier was a hard way of life. When Abe was nine years old, his mother became ill and died. A year later, Abe's father married Sarah Bush. She moved to the cabin and helped raise Abe and his sister.

Why did Abe Lincoln's life change when he was nine years old?

(1) He was raised on the frontier.
(2) His mother died.
(3) His father married Sarah Bush.
(4) He and his sister were raised by Sarah Bush.

In Step 1 you read the question. In Step 2 you read the passage and thought about the question. In Step 3 you answered the question. The correct answer is (2). Abe Lincoln's life changed because his mother died. Choice (1) does not mention a change. Choices (3) and (4) are about changes that happened after Abe Lincoln was nine years old.

Practice the strategy. Use the steps you learned. Circle the
number of the correct answer.

WHAT CAN YOU DO ON THE INTERNET?

The Internet has been called an "Information Superhighway."
There is a huge amount of information on the Internet. For
example, if you want to buy a car, you can view different models
in your price range on the Internet. You can view the car's interior
seats, shown in the color you like. With just a click, you can
change the color. You can also find a home or an apartment
online. Then you can go on a "virtual tour" from your computer.

1. Why is the Internet called an "Information Superhighway"?

(1) You can view cars on the Internet.

(2) You can purchase a car on the Internet.

(3) A great deal of information is available on the Internet.

(4) You can tour an apartment on the Internet.

HOW DOES OPRAH WINFREY SPEND HER TIME?

In the morning, Oprah will tape her TV program—"The
Oprah Winfrey Show." In the afternoon, she will meet with her
staff to plan new shows. She will also meet with people who have
ideas for movies and TV specials. And there are meetings to
decide where Oprah will appear. Then there is the work she does
with children who live in a Chicago housing project.

From *Meet Oprah Winfrey* by Audreen Buffalo

2. What does Oprah Winfrey do in the afternoons?

(1) tapes her show

(2) plans new shows

(3) makes movies

(4) makes appearances

Check your answers on page 153.

Read each passage and question carefully. Circle the number of the correct answer.

Questions 1–3 are based on the following paragraph.

DOES BIRTH ORDER MATTER?

Does it matter if you were born first, second, or third in a family? Does that affect who you are as an adult? Some scientists say "yes." They say that you may have certain traits, or qualities, because of your place in the family. The first-born is often a leader. Parents tend to count on the oldest child. Middle children are peacemakers. They try to bring people together. The youngest child is the charmer but may leave hard problems for others to solve.

1. Based on the question above the paragraph, what could you predict that the paragraph is about?
   - (1) giving birth
   - (2) the order children are born in
   - (3) what matters in life
   - (4) preparing for childbirth

2. Which children are known as peacemakers?
   - (1) the first-born
   - (2) the middle children
   - (3) the youngest children
   - (4) all children

3. Which word or words give a clue to the meaning of *traits*?
   - (1) "try"
   - (2) "charmer"
   - (3) "qualities"
   - (4) "count on"

Questions 4–6 are based on the following passage.

WHAT HAPPENED TO THE *FITZGERALD*?

The S. S. *Edmund Fitzgerald* was a huge carrier. For ten years, it had hauled iron ore across the Great Lakes from Wisconsin to Michigan. It had made the trip hundreds of times when it set out on November 9, 1975. A terrible storm was forecast, and high winds were predicted.

The ship was caught in the storm. The captain of the *Fitzgerald* stayed in touch with another ship. First, he radioed that they had lost their radar. They were also taking on water. Then he radioed, "We are holding our own." That was the *Fitzgerald's* last message. The ship sank without sending a distress signal. All 29 crew members were lost at sea.

4. Which book might have more information about the sinking of the *Fitzgerald*?

(1) *Shipwrecks of the Atlantic*
(2) *Finding the Titanic*
(3) *Shipping Procedures for the Great Lakes*
(4) *Disasters on the Great Lakes*

5. What was the last message from the *Fitzgerald*?

(1) "We are taking on water."
(2) "We have lost our radar."
(3) "We are caught in the storm."
(4) "We are holding our own."

6. In paragraph 1, the word *carrier* means

(1) a person who carries materials, such as the mail.
(2) a company that moves people or goods.
(3) a ship that carries goods from one place to another.
(4) a living thing on which germs travel and cause disease.

WHY IS THE CUCKOO AN UNUSUAL BIRD?

The female cuckoo lays her egg in the nest of other birds. It is up to this other pair of birds to sustain the chick. Surprisingly, many birds do feed the cuckoo chick as if it were their own. When the cuckoo chick becomes larger, it pushes the other chicks from the nest. Still the birds continue to feed it. Once it fledges—grows the feathers needed to fly—the cuckoo finally leaves the nest.

7. You can figure out that *fledges* means

(1) starts out on its own.

(2) grows the feathers needed to fly.

(3) takes over the nest.

(4) grows large.

8. Which definition best fits the word *sustain*?

(1) to endure

(2) to support from below

(3) to provide food for

(4) to make a certain ruling in court

Check your answers on page 153.

Unit 1 Skill Check-Up Chart

Check your answers. In the first column, circle the numbers of any questions that you missed. Then look across the rows to see the skills you need to review and the pages where you can find each skill.

Question	Skill	Page
2, 5	Scanning	12–17
1, 4	Predicting	18–23
3, 7	Using Context Clues	24–31
6, 8	Understanding Multiple Meanings	32–35

Unit 2   Finding the Main Idea

In this unit you will learn about

- finding the stated main idea
- understanding the implied main idea
- finding supporting details

introduction

topic

implied

detail

When you read an article or a book, you see that the writing is broken up into groups of sentences called paragraphs. Paragraphs make writing easier to read.

How many sentences are in the paragraph above?

_____

A paragraph is made up of one or more sentences. All of these sentences tell about a single thought or idea. This single idea is called the main idea.

Why do you think it is important for a paragraph to have only one main idea?

_____

_____

_____

paragraph
a group of one or more sentences about one idea or topic

indented
writing that is set in from the normal starting place

You read many different kinds of materials, such as books or articles in a magazine or newspaper. Most written material is made up of **paragraphs**. A paragraph is a group of sentences. The sentences in a paragraph are all about the same idea.

It is easy to tell where new paragraphs begin. Most paragraphs begin with a sentence that is **indented**. Sometimes paragraphs are separated from each other by extra space.

Count the number of paragraphs in this article. Then write the number on the line below.

In most states, the insurance company of the person who causes a car accident pays all the bills. Therefore, it is important to know who caused the accident. That person is said to be at fault.

Some states have no-fault car insurance. This means that it doesn't matter who caused the accident. Each person's insurance company pays his or her own bills.

Even in a no-fault accident, one driver can still sue the other. The person whose car was hit may sue the other driver. Passengers in the car that was hit may also sue. People are most likely to sue when there has been an injury.

This article contains _____ paragraphs.

Ideas are easier to understand when they are broken up into paragraphs. Each paragraph is about one main thought or idea. A new paragraph may give new and different information about the subject. Or it may begin a new idea altogether.

Check your answer on page 153.

The main idea, or **topic**, tells what a paragraph is about. Look back at the passage on page 44. Each paragraph in the passage has its own main idea. The first paragraph tells how insurance companies pay for car accidents in states with at-fault insurance. The second paragraph tells how insurance companies pay for car accidents in states with no-fault insurance. The third paragraph tells about drivers and passengers who sue after car accidents.

topic
the subject, or main idea

Not all groups of sentences are paragraphs. To make up a paragraph, a group of sentences must make sense together. If the sentences do not tell about the same idea, they don't make up a paragraph.

Read these two groups of sentences. Decide which one is a paragraph with one main idea. Circle the number of the correct answer.

(1)   New jobs are created every day, but people need training for these jobs. They need new skills. To get these skills, people may have to go back to school. This can be hard for many people. They do not have the time or the money to go back to school. The government should help. It should set up a job-training program that pays people to get the skills they need.

(2)   A rainbow is made up of seven colors. They are red, orange, yellow, green, blue, indigo, and violet. A pink room makes people edgy. A red one makes them excited. Many animals can't see colors. Dogs don't see colors as clearly as humans do. Paints can be mixed to form different colors.

The first group of sentences is a paragraph. This group of sentences tells about one main idea, or topic. The topic is **limited** to a few things about the subject. All of the sentences are about job training.

limited
not everything about the subject is included or explained

Check your answer on page 153.

The second group of sentences on page 45 is not a paragraph. All of the sentences talk about color, but the topic is not limited. The sentences discuss many different ideas about color. No one idea stands out. That's because this group of sentences has more than one topic.

There is usually one sentence in a paragraph that states the main idea. The main idea is often found in the first sentence.

Read this paragraph. Then underline the sentence that tells the main idea.

There is a growing health care problem in the United States. The cost of health care keeps going up. Some employers can no longer pay the entire cost of a worker's health insurance. They pass on some of the expense to their workers. Some workers can't afford to pay these added costs. As a result, they may turn down the insurance even though they need it. They can't afford to have any more money taken from their paychecks.

The sentence that tells what the paragraph is about is called the **topic sentence**. The main idea is stated in this sentence. All of the other sentences support and help explain the main idea.

Sometimes the topic sentence is not the first sentence of a paragraph. It may be a sentence in the middle of the paragraph. When the topic sentence is in the middle, it often follows a short **introduction**. The introduction is meant to get your attention. It might create suspense or remind you of something you already know. The introduction tries to interest you enough to keep you reading.

Check your answer on page 153.

topic sentence
the sentence that gives the main idea of the paragraph

introduction
a book or a paragraph's beginning that prepares people for what they will read

In the following paragraph, the topic sentence is not the first sentence. The topic sentence follows an introduction. As you read, think about the paragraph's main idea and find the topic sentence.

Read the following paragraph. Then answer the questions.

Some people say it's boring. Some say it's just for grandmas. Others say it's a waste of time. But are these opinions out of date? Many people today think that knitting is just plain cool. And it isn't just the older folks who think this. The hobby has taken hold among people of all ages—teens, college students, and adults. Stars think it's cool, too. Julia Roberts, Daryl Hannah, and Bridget Fonda are three actors who like to sit back, relax, and knit.

1. Write the topic sentence of the paragraph.

   _____

   _____

2. Write two sentences that support the paragraph's main idea.

   _____

   _____

   _____

   _____

As you read the first four sentences, you may have wondered what the paragraph was about. Some opinions are given, but you don't know what is being described. To find out, you read on. These first four sentences are the introduction. They lead you to the topic sentence. By the time you find out what the paragraph is about, your interest is high and you are ready to read more.

Check your answers on page 154.

Sometimes the topic sentence is the last sentence of a paragraph. The sentences in the paragraph build up to the topic sentence. This may make the paragraph more exciting. The topic sentence may also be the last sentence of a paragraph because the paragraph is presenting a series of events that caused something to happen. When the topic sentence is near the end of the paragraph, the details come first. They lead you to the main idea.

Read the following paragraph. As you read, think about the topic sentence and the main idea. Then answer the questions.

In 1955 a black woman, Rosa Parks, refused to give up a seat to a white person on a bus in Montgomery, Alabama. In the uproar that followed, blacks refused to ride the Montgomery buses until they could sit anywhere they chose. For a year Montgomery blacks walked or carpooled. The city buses lost money and finally had to agree to black demands. In 1956 the Supreme Court said blacks must have equal access to all interstate buses.

From *America Alive* by Jean Karl

1. Underline the topic sentence.
2. Write one sentence from the paragraph that tells more about the paragraph's main idea.

_____

_____

GED Tip

As you practice reading passages for the GED Test, underline the topic sentence of each paragraph. This will help you understand the main idea of the paragraph.

In the paragraph above, the sentences lead up to the topic sentence. They present a series of events. First, Rosa Parks refused to give up her seat on the bus. Next, African Americans refused to ride the buses. The city buses lost money.

These sentences tell about events that caused something to happen. The events caused the Supreme Court to make a decision. The paragraph's main idea is that the Supreme Court said blacks have to have equal access to buses. The last sentence of the paragraph is the topic sentence. All of the other sentences support and relate to that sentence.

Check your answers on page 154.

Practice

Read the paragraphs and answer the questions.

(1)   Most accidents happen at home. Try to avoid such injuries. Don't put butter on b_____ ____n't move a person who has been seriously injured ___ ____ ____ once I was injured. No one moved me. ___ ____ ____ d me calling for help. Then I had to wait more than two hours at the ____spital.

_____ ____ ____u can do to help a person who ____ ____ get medical help right away. ____ ____ ____es. Follow any directions they give you ____ ____ ____ They may tell you not to move the ____ ____ ____ you to cover the person with a ____ ____ ____ and do what they tell you.

____ ____ groups of sentences is a paragraph? Circle the number of the correct answer.

2. Write the topic sentence of the paragraph you chose.

_____

_____

3. Find the topic sentence in the following paragraph. Then write the topic sentence on the lines below.

     The date was February 20, 1962. The place was Cape Canaveral, Florida. John Glenn was strapped into his seat. Glenn was about to travel in space around Earth. It was something no American had ever done before. The countdown began: Ten, nine, eight, seven, six, five, four, three, two, one, blast off! Huge flames shot out of the rocket, and the spacecraft began to rise.

_____

_____

_____

Check your answers on page 154.

stated
written or spoken

implied
unwritten or unspoken

In some paragraphs, the main idea is easy to find. It is **stated** clearly in the topic sentence. However, not all paragraphs have a topic sentence that directly states what the paragraph is about.

A main idea that is not stated directly is called an **implied** main idea. Although no topic sentence states the main idea, all the sentences in the paragraph hint at the main idea. When the main idea is not stated, you need to use the hints the sentences give you. First, think about how all the sentences are related. Then ask yourself what the paragraph is mostly about. That is the main idea.

Read the following paragraph. Then answer the question.

Eloy Flores is a single parent. He gets his two children dressed and fed before he leaves for work. Then he drops them off at the day care center. When Eloy works late, he nervously checks his watch. He has to be at the day care center no later than 6:30. After he picks up his children, he heads home and cooks dinner. He gives the children a bath and has them in bed by 9:00. After doing the dishes, Eloy watches TV. If he has the energy, he plays his banjo. Then he gets ready for the next day. He packs lunches and does laundry. The next morning, Eloy begins his day all over again.

Which sentence tells the main idea of the paragraph? Circle the number of the correct answer.

(1) Eloy gets his children dressed and fed each morning.
(2) Eloy doesn't have much time to practice the banjo.
(3) Eloy prepares meals for his family.
(4) Eloy spends his time working and caring for his children.

You can see that the paragraph does not have one sentence that states the main idea. The main idea is implied.

Check your answer on page 154.

Read the following paragraphs and answer the questions.

Phyllis works out each day. During the summer, she swims and jogs. In the winter, she walks at the indoor track at the community center. She also watches how much fat she eats. She reads the labels on foods. She eats a lot of fresh fruits and vegetables.

1. Which sentence states the main idea of the paragraph? Circle the number of the correct answer.

(1) Phyllis likes to swim and jog.

(2) Phyllis likes to walk in the winter and swim in the summer.

(3) Phyllis takes good care of herself by exercising and watching what she eats.

(4) Phyllis likes to read the labels on foods.

Fax machines send information across town or around the world in just a few minutes. They allow businesses to get information to their customers quickly. Cell phones allow salespeople to call customers from their cars and keep in touch with their office. Plumbers, electricians, and other service workers use pagers to let customers reach them quickly.

2. Which sentence states the main idea of the paragraph? Circle the number of the correct answer.

(1) Cell phones have many uses.

(2) Technology helps people do their jobs.

(3) All businesses need pagers and cell phones.

(4) Too much technology is bad for business.

GED Tip

If you read a paragraph on the GED Test and the main idea is not stated directly, ask yourself what the paragraph is mostly about. That is the main idea.

It was 1975 in a large city in China. Animals had been acting strangely. Experts saw this odd behavior and believed it meant an earthquake would soon take place. Chinese officials told people this prediction and ordered them to leave the city. Within three days, there was a huge earthquake.

3. Write the paragraph's implied main idea on the lines.

_____

_____

Check your answers on page 154.

Practice

Read each paragraph. Decide which sentence is the topic sentence. Circle the number of the correct answer.

1.   There is help for people who feel that they have been treated unfairly by a business. If you feel that you have been cheated in any way, look in the phone book. Call the consumer-protection agency in your city. The people there will tell you about laws that can help you. You don't have to go to a lawyer. Check with government agencies first. They will probably be able to help you—for free!

    (1) There is help for people who feel that they have been treated unfairly by a business.

    (2) They will probably be able to help you—for free!

    (3) You don't have to go to a lawyer.

    (4) There is no topic sentence.

2.   Some people were not pleased when President Franklin D. Roosevelt spent public money on his dog, Fala. Roosevelt said, "I don't resent attacks, but Fala does resent them." The public loved him for saying this. President Richard Nixon said he would never give up his dog, Checkers. Some people think this was one of the reasons he was chosen to run as Vice President. President Lyndon Johnson once picked up his dogs by their ears. He got many angry letters about what he had done.

    (1) President Richard Nixon said he would never give up his dog, Checkers.

    (2) President Lyndon Johnson once picked up his dogs by their ears.

    (3) Some people were not pleased when President Franklin D. Roosevelt spent public money on his dog, Fala.

    (4) There is no topic sentence.

3.   You'll probably have difficulty sleeping. You may have headaches. You'll also cough. You may cough more than you did when you were smoking. That's because your lungs are trying to clear out years of built-up tar. You may feel a tingling or a numbness in different parts of your body. This is because your blood circulation is improving. Your heartbeat might also slow down. Your blood pressure is sure to be lower as well.

(1)   You'll probably have difficulty sleeping.

(2)   You'll also cough.

(3)   Your blood pressure is sure to be lower as well.

(4)   There is no topic sentence.

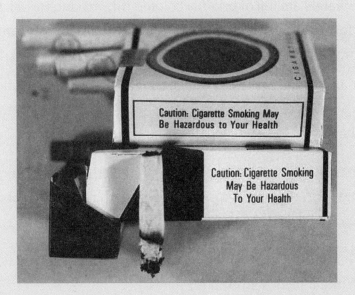

Read the paragraph. Then answer the question.

4.   Some people like to be scared at the movies. Others look for the magic of romance. Some like a good science fiction adventure. Many people like to laugh and look forward to comedies. Westerns have become rare, but they are still well liked. Kids enjoy animated movies. Some people will go out of their way to see a foreign film. People have different tastes, but it seems everyone loves movies.

Write the topic sentence on the lines.

_____

_____

Check your answers on page 154.

As you have learned, the main idea of a paragraph tells what the paragraph is mostly about. There is more to a paragraph than the main idea, though. The other sentences explain, **prove**, or give more information about the main idea. These sentences are called **supporting details**.

prove
show that something is true

supporting details
details that explain, prove, or give information about the main idea

Read the following paragraph. The main idea can be found in the first sentence.

Hawaii is a great vacation spot. Hawaii sits in the clear, blue waters of the Pacific. White beaches stretch for miles. The waters are full of brightly colored fish, making Hawaii a perfect place for scuba divers. If you like nightlife, there are plenty of clubs and restaurants.

The main idea is that Hawaii is a great place to go on vacation. How do the other sentences support the main idea? They tell about things that might make you want to visit the islands.

The first sentence of the paragraph tells the main idea. The remaining sentences are supporting details that tell more about the main idea. Three of these supporting details are

- Hawaii sits in the clear, blue waters of the Pacific.
- White beaches stretch for miles.
- The waters are full of brightly colored fish, making Hawaii a perfect place for scuba divers.

Write another supporting detail from the paragraph.

_____

_____

These four details explain, prove, and give more information about the main idea that Hawaii is a great vacation spot.

Check your answer on page 155.

Supporting details give you information about the main idea. All of the sentences in the paragraph about Hawaii prove the point that Hawaii is a great place to go on a vacation. They also answer these questions:

- Where is Hawaii?
- What can you do there?
- What are the beaches like?

Supporting details have two purposes. One purpose is to explain or prove the main idea. The other purpose is to give more information about the main idea. In both cases, the details support the main idea. They help make the main idea clear. Supporting details may also make it easier to understand or accept the main idea.

Read the paragraph. Then answer the questions below.

There are many ways to cook vegetables. You can steam them. You can boil them. You can bake them or fry them. You can grill them over an open fire at the same time as another part of your meal. Steamed, baked, and grilled vegetables keep more of their vitamins than boiled vegetables. Fried vegetables keep their vitamins, too, but they are high in fat.

1. What is the main idea of the paragraph?

_____

_____

2. List one detail that helps prove the main idea.

_____

_____

3. List one detail that gives information about the main idea.

_____

_____

GED Tip

The answers to questions about supporting details can often be found by scanning the passage for key words used in the question.

Check your answers on page 155.

Questions 1–3 are based on the following paragraph.

Putting an ad in the personals column of a newspaper can be an easy and safe way to meet interesting people. My older sister met her husband this way. You just run the ad and wait for the letters to come. After reading the letters, you decide who you want to meet. You can meet the person for the first time in a coffee shop or other well-lighted public place. This person never has to know your telephone number, where you live, or even your last name. You can get to know each other first. Then you can decide whether to see each other again—with no hard feelings.

> Nice guy with good job, brown hair, hazel eyes, 6 ft. tall, on heavy side, age 32. My problem is I can't find the right girl. Maybe it's you.
>
> Box J3014

1. Write the topic sentence on the lines.

   _____

   _____

   _____

Circle the number of the correct answer.

2. What do the supporting details in the paragraph tell you?

   (1) why personal ads are safe

   (2) why personal ads are easy

   (3) how to answer personal ads

   (4) both (1) and (2)

3. Which of these would <u>not</u> be a safe place to meet someone who answers your personal ad?

   (1) a coffee shop

   (2) a well-lighted public place

   (3) your house or apartment

   (4) all of the above

Small claims courts settle disagreements that involve small amounts of money. Suppose a woman sells you a used washing machine. She tells you that it's only five years old and that it works fine. When you get it home, you find out that the washing machine doesn't work. If the woman refuses to give your money back, you can sue her in small claims court. To file a claim, you need the name and address of the person you want to sue. You also need proof that you have a good reason to sue. In most states, the fees for filing a claim are small, and you don't even need a lawyer.

Circle the number of the correct answer.

4. Which of these is the topic sentence in the paragraph?

(1) the first sentence
(2) the fourth sentence
(3) the last sentence
(4) There is no topic sentence.

5. A small claims court would settle disagreements that involved

(1) any amount of money.
(2) small amounts of money.
(3) washing machines.
(4) used items.

6. Which detail explains that it won't cost much to file a claim?

(1) You also need proof that you have a good reason to sue.
(2) To file a claim, you need the name and address of the person you want to sue.
(3) If the woman refuses to give your money back, you can sue her in small claims court.
(4) In most states, the fees for filing a claim are small, and you don't even need a lawyer.

Check your answers on page 155.

GED Skill Strategy

Understanding Main Ideas

Some paragraphs have a sentence that states the main idea. This is called the topic sentence. In many paragraphs, the first sentence is the topic sentence. In other paragraphs, the topic sentence comes later in the paragraph.

 Strategy Read the paragraph. Ask yourself: What is this paragraph about? Which sentence tells the main idea?

1. Look for a sentence that ties all of the other sentences together.

2. Remember that the topic sentence can be anywhere in the paragraph.

Exercise 1: Underline the topic sentence in each paragraph.

1. We exercise and lift light weights. We eat whole grains and fruits and vegetables. We eat less fat. Everyone is trying to lose weight. Getting healthy is a great goal for all of us.

2. The key to moving into a new home is good organization. The first thing to do is to decide when you want to move. Call the mover as soon as possible to set the date. Or you can call a truck rental company if you want to do all the work yourself. Tell them which day you want to rent a truck. Next, start packing. Mark each of your boxes with the name of the room where it belongs. This will limit how many times you have to move heavy boxes.

3. Sometimes the weather turns out to be the opposite of what was predicted. Even experts who have years of experience can find it difficult to forecast the weather. Computers can help. They are filled with data about weather patterns. They can tell what kind of weather is likely. Their prediction could be right. But it could also be wrong. Weather forecasting is not an exact science.

Sometimes paragraphs do not have a topic sentence. The main idea is suggested, rather than stated. These paragraphs have implied main ideas. The following paragraph does not have a topic sentence. What is the implied main idea?

> One symptom of a heart attack is pain in your chest. Another is shortness of breath. Some people also have pain in their arms or in their necks.

The main idea of the paragraph is that a heart attack can have several symptoms.

 Strategy Read the paragraph. Ask yourself: Is there a topic sentence that tells the main idea? If not, how can I figure it out?
1. Think about what each sentence, or supporting detail, is about.
2. Ask yourself: How do the sentences relate to each other?

Exercise 2: Choose the implied main idea for each paragraph. Circle the letter of the correct answer.

4. One type of volcano is called an active volcano. It shows signs of volcanic action. Another type is the dormant volcano. This type of volcano hasn't erupted in a long time. The third type is the extinct volcano. It hasn't erupted in hundreds of years. Scientists think it may never erupt again. They consider this type of volcano to be dead.

(a) Volcanoes are always a threat to people.
(b) There are three types of volcanoes.

5. The crowd laughed at Dani's performance. She told funny jokes. She did impressions that made fun of famous people. She walked into the crowd and let people ask her questions. Then she gave quick, funny answers. The crowd roared with laughter.

(a) The crowd loved Dani's performance.
(b) Dani's performance shocked the crowd.

Check your answers on page 155.

Using the GED Purpose Question

On the GED Reading Test, you read passages and then answer questions about each passage. Before every passage there is a question in dark type called a purpose question. One strategy for understanding GED passages is to think about the purpose question as you read.

 Strategy   Try this strategy with the following example. Use these steps.

Step 1   Read the purpose question. What is it asking?

Step 2   Read the passage. Think about the purpose question.

Step 3   Answer the multiple-choice question.

WHAT IS THE CITY COUNCIL BEING ASKED TO DO?

A hot issue was put before the West Springs City Council on Monday. The owners of ten homes just outside the western edge of town want their property connected to the city water system.

"It's only ten homes," said West Springs resident Ann Johnson. "They should be connected. Those people are part of the city even if they live outside the boundary. Their kids go to West Spring School. They play ball at the West Springs Youth Center."

Which of the following is the issue before the city council?

   (1) Should the city provide water to all the homes in the area?

   (2) Should kids who live outside the city use the local youth center?

   (3) Should the city provide water to ten homes outside the city?

   (4) Should kids who live outside the city go to West Springs School?

In Step 1 you read the purpose question. In Step 2 you read the passage and thought about the purpose question. In Step 3 you answered the multiple-choice question. The correct answer is (3). This answer is supported by the details in the passage. Choice (1) is about all homes, not ten. Choices (2) and (4) are not supported by the passage.

Practice the strategy. Use the steps you learned. Circle the number of the correct answer.

HOW DID DOGS AND HUMANS BECOME FRIENDS?

How did dogs begin to be part of human lives? Long ago, dogs roamed human camps looking for food scraps. This helped keep the camp clean. As dogs and people lived around each other, they got to know each other. People valued dogs that barked when a stranger came near. They liked having dogs to protect them. Dogs were also valuable to early hunters. The dogs' sense of smell helped them track animals.

1. What did dogs offer early humans?

   (1) a bark that frightened animals away
   (2) help with cleanliness, protection, and hunting
   (3) friendship and a desire to please
   (4) love of strangers

WHAT DO THE STARS AND STRIPES STAND FOR?

The first United States flag had thirteen stars and thirteen stripes. In 1794, two new states became part of the country. Two new stars and two new stripes were added to the flag. More states soon became part of the country. Congress realized that the flag would look strange with too many stars and stripes. They decided that the flag would have only thirteen stripes. These would stand for the original thirteen colonies that became the first states. There would be a star for each state. When a new state joined the country, a new star would be added to the flag.

2. What do the stripes on the United States flag stand for?

   (1) They stand for each state in the Union.
   (2) They stand for the first fifteen states.
   (3) They stand for each new state that is added.
   (4) They stand for the original thirteen colonies.

Check your answers on page 156.

Read each paragraph and question carefully. Circle the number of the correct answer.

Questions 1–3 are based on the following paragraph.

DOES CLEANLINESS COUNT?

If you have a cold, you may cover your mouth when you cough. This protects people from your germs. But if you then touch food as you prepare dinner, you may spread your cold to anyone who eats the meal. People should wash their hands after touching their eyes, nose, or mouth. Ask any restaurant owner. Ask a doctor or a nurse. Hand washing helps prevent the spread of germs.

1. What is the main idea of the paragraph?

   (1) Cover your mouth when you cough.
   (2) Hand washing helps prevent the spread of germs.
   (3) This protects people from your germs.
   (4) Ask a doctor or nurse about germs.

2. What can happen if you prepare dinner without washing your hands?

   (1) You may protect people from germs.
   (2) You may spread your germs to others.
   (3) You may catch a cold.
   (4) You may need to talk to a doctor or nurse.

3. What should you do after rubbing your eyes?

   (1) Cover your mouth.
   (2) Talk to a doctor or nurse.
   (3) Wash your hands.
   (4) Ask someone else to prepare dinner.

Questions 4–6 are based on the following paragraph.

WHAT IS IN *THE OLD FARMER'S ALMANAC*?

In *The Old Farmer's Almanac*, you'll find weather predictions for the coming year. Tables tell when the sun will rise each day. You can learn about the year's phases of the moon. You can read about how to dig a well and line it with stones. You'll find an answer to why some people prefer to live in the city while others like the country best. You'll see when eclipses will happen in the coming year. You'll even find advice on how to get rid of nasty weeds.

4. What is the main idea of the paragraph?

  (1) *The Old Farmer's Almanac* offers information, predictions, and advice.

  (2) *The Old Farmer's Almanac* tells you how to dig a well and gives advice.

  (3) Plan your days based on the weather predictions in *The Old Farmer's Almanac*.

  (4) *The Old Farmer's Almanac* explains why the city is better than the country.

5. Which of the following is a supporting detail?

  (1) You'll even find advice on how to get rid of nasty weeds.

  (2) You'll find weather predictions for the coming year.

  (3) You can learn about the year's phases of the moon.

  (4) all of the above

6. Which of these is something that you would find in *The Old Farmer's Almanac*?

  (1) list of homes that are for sale in the country

  (2) the exact weather conditions for the weekend

  (3) maps of different countries

  (4) the year's phases of the moon

Questions 7–8 are based on the following paragraph.

HOW DO YOU REGISTER FOR CLASSES?

It's easy to sign up for a class at the Art Center. First, decide which class you want to take. Then complete the form at the back of the course catalog. Write your name, address, phone number, and the name of the class you want to take. Send your form and payment to the address in the catalog.

7. What is the topic sentence of the paragraph?

(1) First, decide which class you want to take.

(2) Write your name, address, phone number, and the name of the class you want to take.

(3) It's easy to sign up for a class at the Art Center.

(4) Then complete the form at the back of the course catalog.

8. What is the last thing you should do?

(1) Decide which class you want to take.

(2) Complete the form at the back of the course catalog.

(3) Write the name of the class you want to take.

(4) Send your form and payment to the address in the catalog.

Check your answers on page 156.

Unit 2 Skill Check-Up Chart

Check your answers. In the first column, circle the numbers of any questions that you missed. Then look across the rows to see the skills you need to review and the pages where you can find each skill.

Question	Skill	Page
1, 7	Finding the Stated Main Idea	44–49
4	Understanding the Implied Main Idea	50–53
2, 3, 5, 6, 8	Finding Supporting Details	54–57

Organizing Ideas

In this unit you will learn about

- showing time order
- comparing and contrasting
- showing cause and effect
- giving examples

contrast

illustrate

cause

phrase

Paragraphs are organized in many ways. They can show how two things are alike or different. They can show how one thing caused something else to happen. Knowing how the ideas in a paragraph are organized helps you understand the paragraph's main point.

List two ways that you and a friend are alike.

_____

_____

Another way a paragraph can be organized is in the order that things happen or should be done. Words like *first* and *then* help you know the order of things.

List two things you did to get ready this morning in the order that you did them.

_____

_____

organized
arranged in a certain way

sequence
the order in which things are done or happen

chronological order
arranged in order by time—what happened first, second, third, and so on

To understand a paragraph, you need to know its main idea. Then you can find details that tell more about the main idea. Another way to understand a paragraph is to look at how it is **organized**. The organization lets you know how the ideas fit together.

There are many ways writers organize a paragraph. One way is to show the order in which things are done or happen. This is called **sequence**. One type of sequence is called **chronological order**.

Chronological order is also called time order. Time order tells about events that happen. The writer starts with what happens first, then what happens next, and so on, until the final event.

In the paragraph below, the topic sentence comes first. Notice that after the topic sentence, all of the supporting details tell about Lisa's busy morning. The details tell what Lisa did in chronological order.

Read the paragraph and answer the questions. Write your answers on the lines.

(1) Lisa had a busy morning before her job interview. (2) First, she got dressed. (3) Then she made breakfast. (4) Next, she walked to the bus stop. (5) Finally, an hour later, she arrived for her interview.

1. Which sentence tells what happened first?

_____

2. Which sentence tells what happened second?

_____

3. Which sentence tells what happened third?

_____

4. Which sentence tells what happened last?

_____

Check your answers on page 157.

Some words in a paragraph can help you figure out time order. These clue words or **phrases** tell the order in which events happen. Some common time-order clue words and phrases are *first, second, then, next, before, after, yesterday, today, finally,* and *at last.*

phrase
a group of two or more words, but not a complete sentence

Read the paragraph on page 66 again. Write three words that are clues about time order.

_____

You should have written three of these words: *first, then, next,* and *finally.* These words tell about time order. Some paragraphs contain other clues about time order. Dates (March 10), years (2004), and times of day (9:00 A.M.) are also clues that let you know the order in which things happen.

Stories and articles are often written in time order. They tell the order in which events happened. Recipes and other directions also follow time order. They tell the order in which the steps in a process should be done.

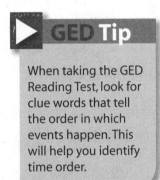
GED Tip

When taking the GED Reading Test, look for clue words that tell the order in which events happen. This will help you identify time order.

Read the paragraph.

Making a Bookshelf

First, measure the area where you want to put the shelf. Second, plan how you want the shelf to look. Draw a rough plan. After that, buy the materials you need. Finally, begin working. Remember to take your time.

List four clue words or phrases that tell you these directions are organized in time order.

1. _____

2. _____

3. _____

4. _____

Check your answers on page 157.

Read the following passage.

> One day in 1943, a farmer in western Mexico noticed that a small hill had grown in his cornfield. The next day, the hill was bigger. A few days later, he saw that there was a crack in the hill. Then hot gas started coming out of the crack. Thirty minutes later, there was an explosion. A cloud of gas and ash shot miles into the air!
>
> The explosion continued, and soon the whole village was covered with lava and volcanic ash. Today, Paricutín is a volcano 1,345 feet high. It stands where the cornfield and village used to be.

Answer the questions.

1. Write three clue words or phrases that show the paragraphs are organized in time order.

   _____

   _____

   _____

2. What happened first?

   _____

   _____

3. What happened after hot gas started coming out of the crack in the hill?

   _____

   _____

Questions 4–6 are based on the following passage.

Today, cities in the United States are growing bigger and bigger. Some people say that one day the northeastern seacoast will be one big city. They say this will happen because it is hard to make a living on a small farm. Many farmers are selling their land to big companies and moving to cities to find work.

At first, city growth happened slowly. In 1800, only one out of every ten people lived in a city. In 1900, four out of ten people lived in a city. After 1900, more and more people came to the United States. Most of them moved to the cities, too. By 1916, almost half of the people in the United States lived in a city. By 2000, about eight out of ten people lived in or near a city.

Circle the number of the correct answer.

4. How do you know that paragraph 2 is organized in time order?

   (1) It tells how many people lived in cities in 1900.
   (2) It tells about city growth over a period of years.
   (3) It tells about life in U.S. cities.
   (4) It tells how many people live in or near a city today.

5. Which of the following is the most recent fact in the passage?

   (1) Four of ten people lived in a city.
   (2) Almost half of the people in the United States lived in cities.
   (3) Only one out of every ten people lived in a city.
   (4) About eight out of ten people lived in or near a city.

6. When did almost half of the people in the U.S. live in cities?

   (1) 1800
   (2) 1900
   (3) 1916
   (4) 2000

Check your answers on page 157.

compare
showing how things are alike

contrast
showing how things are different

Paragraphs can be organized in many different ways. One way is by using time order. Another way is by showing how two things are alike. This way is called **comparing**. Paragraphs may also show how two things are different. This is called **contrasting**.

Sometimes the same paragraph will both compare and contrast. It will describe the likenesses and differences between two things. Clue words can help you tell when a paragraph is comparing or contrasting.

Clue Words that Compare	Clue Words that Contrast
(How are things alike?)	**(How are things different?)**
■ alike	■ different
■ like	■ unlike
■ similar	■ but
■ too	■ yet
■ both	■ however
■ also	■ more
■ same	■ less
■ likewise	■ on the other hand

Read the paragraph.

Snorkeling and scuba diving are alike in some ways and different in others. Both are water sports. For both you need fins and a mask. However, when you snorkel, you float on the surface of the water. You breathe air through your snorkel. When you scuba dive, you go under the water. You can stay there for twenty minutes or more. This means you need an air tank and other equipment. Scuba diving can be dangerous. You have to take classes and pass a test before you can dive. On the other hand, you need almost no training to snorkel. It is less dangerous.

Look back on page 70 at the paragraph about snorkeling and scuba diving. The first sentence is the topic sentence. The words *alike* and *different* are found in this sentence. These words tell you that two or more things will be compared and contrasted.

List the clue words used in the paragraph on page 70.

Words that compare

_____

Words that contrast

_____

_____

These clue words help you see how snorkeling and scuba diving are alike and different. The paragraph is organized by comparing and contrasting these two things. First, the paragraph tells how the two sports are alike.

Alike

■ Both are water sports
■ Both use fins and mask

Then the paragraph tells how the two sports are different.

Different

Snorkeling	Scuba Diving
■ Breathe through snorkel	■ Need air tank
■ Stay on surface	■ Can stay under water 20 minutes
■ Not very dangerous	■ Can be dangerous
■ Almost no training needed	■ Need to take classes and test

GED Tip

When taking the GED Reading Test, look for words that compare or contrast. This will help you answer questions about how things are alike and how they are different.

Check your answers on page 157.

Questions 1–3 are based on the following paragraph.

> The lives of two famous presidents were strangely alike in many ways. Abraham Lincoln was elected to Congress in 1847. Exactly 100 years later, John F. Kennedy was also elected to Congress. Both men became president 13 years after being elected to Congress. Both men were killed while they were president. Both were warned by their secretaries not to go to the place where they were killed. The last name of Lincoln's secretary was Kennedy. The last name of Kennedy's secretary was Lincoln. The man who killed Lincoln was shot before he could go to trial. So was the man who killed Kennedy. The vice president was the new leader after each man died. Both vice presidents had the same last name—Johnson.

Circle the number of the correct answer.

1. This paragraph tells

    (1) how the lives of Lincoln and Kennedy were alike.
    (2) how the lives of Lincoln and Kennedy were different.
    (3) only about Kennedy.
    (4) only about Lincoln.

Answer the questions.

2. Write the topic sentence of the paragraph.

    _____

    _____

3. The paragraph is organized by comparing two presidents. Write the clue words that show this type of organization.

    _____

    _____

Questions 4–6 are based on the following paragraph.

> Babies need food that is very different from the food that adults need. First of all, babies need more fat in their diet than adults do. This is because fat helps the growth of the nervous system. Also, babies do not eat much solid food. They eat mostly breast milk or formula during their first year. Adults, on the other hand, do not need to eat as much fat as babies. Adults need to eat a variety of foods to keep healthy.

Circle the number of the correct answer.

4. Which sentence gives you the first clue that two things are being contrasted?

   (1) the first sentence
   (2) the second sentence
   (3) the fourth sentence
   (4) the sixth sentence

5. Look back at the sentence that you chose in question 4. What word or phrase in the sentence shows that two things are being contrasted?

   (1) first of all
   (2) also
   (3) on the other hand
   (4) different

6. What two things are being contrasted?

   (1) the nervous systems of babies and adults
   (2) the two ways that babies grow
   (3) the kind of milk that babies and adults drink
   (4) the kinds of food babies and adults need

Check your answers on page 157.

cause
why something happens

effect
a result or outcome;
what happens

Los Angeles on January 1, 1994

Some paragraphs are organized by describing something that happens and telling why it happens. This is called **cause** and **effect**. Suppose you are baking a cake, and you leave the cake in the oven too long. What happens? The cake burns. Why did this happen? The cake was left in the oven too long. That is the cause. Burning the cake is the effect.

Read the paragraph. Then answer the question.

> The earth shifts and moves. Shock waves travel in many directions. Buildings shake and streets crack. This is what happens when there is an earthquake.

What is one effect of an earthquake?

_____

_____

The paragraph tells what happens during an earthquake and why. What happens is the effect—the earth shifts and moves, shock waves travel in many directions, buildings shake, and streets crack. Why this happens is the cause—there is an earthquake.

The details in this paragraph are organized to show cause and effect. One thing caused other things to happen. Clue words and phrases often help show cause and effect. Some clue words and phrases are *so, so that, cause, effect, result, because, as a result, therefore, reason, if,* and *consequently.*

Read the paragraph. Circle the clue word or phrase that shows cause and effect.

> Gary forgot to set the alarm clock. He woke up later than usual. As a result, he was late for work.

Check your answers on page 158.

Read the passage below. Then answer the questions.

For some time, Los Angeles has been famous for its cars, freeways, and smog. Southern California has had an air pollution problem for many years. It was first noticed in the 1940's when some crops in the area were blighted[1]. By the 1950's, scientists decided that cars were the biggest cause of ozone[2] smog. Soon after this, California had an air pollution control plan.

The controls were some of the strictest in the world. The plan has helped. Today, the air is cleaner but there are still problems. For example, the amount of ozone in the air over Los Angeles is often three times higher than the EPA limit.

From *The Environment at Risk*
by the National Issues Forums Institute

[1] damaged
[2] a type of oxygen

1. What are the clue words in the first paragraph that tell about cause and effect?

   _____

Look through the paragraphs. Find the causes for each effect.

2. effect: Crops in the Los Angeles area were blighted.

   cause: _____

   _____

3. effect: California had an air pollution control plan.

   cause: _____

   _____

4. effect: Today the air is cleaner.

   cause: _____

   _____

GED Tip

Some questions on the GED Reading Test ask what happened or why. To answer these questions, look for words or phrases that show cause and effect.

Check your answers on page 158.

Questions 1–3 are based on the following paragraph.

> Did you know that owning a pet can help you live longer? High blood pressure and stress are two of the major causes of heart attacks. Some doctors believe that having a pet may help people lower their blood pressure. Having pets may also reduce feelings of stress. Research has shown that when people pat and speak to their pets, their blood pressure drops. Watching fish in a fish tank can have the same results. Pets seem to help people relax and forget about their problems. As a result, stress is reduced, and along with it, the risk of having a heart attack.

Circle the number of the correct answer.

1. How can owning a pet be good for you?

    (1) It lowers blood pressure.
    (2) It reduces feelings of stress.
    (3) It reduces the risk of having a heart attack.
    (4) all of the above

2. Which clue word or phrase shows you that this paragraph is organized by using cause and effect?

    (1) because
    (2) reason
    (3) As a result
    (4) all of the above

3. "... blood pressure drops" is the effect. What is the cause?

    (1) feelings of stress
    (2) when people pat and speak to their pets
    (3) the risk of having a heart attack
    (4) both (1) and (2)

Everyone should have an aloe plant in the kitchen. This plant can help treat burns. If you burn yourself while cooking, break open one of the leaves of the plant. Inside you will see a greenish gel. Rub the gel over the burn. The pain will lessen or stop almost immediately. As a result of using aloe, the burn will not blister. It will also heal faster.

Circle the number of the correct answer.

4. What is the main idea of this paragraph?

   (1) The aloe plant can help treat burns.
   (2) If you cook, you might burn yourself.
   (3) The leaves of the aloe plant break open easily.
   (4) Aloe gel prevents burns from blistering.

5. "Rub the gel over the burn" is the cause. What is the effect?

   (1) The leaf of your aloe plant will break open.
   (2) The burn will disappear immediately.
   (3) The pain will lessen or stop almost immediately.
   (4) all of the above

6. What clue word or phrase tells you that this paragraph is organized by cause and effect?

   (1) If
   (2) Inside
   (3) As a result
   (4) both (1) and (3)

Check your answers on page 158.

illustrate
make clear, explain, or
give examples

One way to prove a point or **illustrate** the main idea is to give examples. Clues can help you see when a writer is giving examples. Some clue words and phrases are *suppose, for example,* and *an example of this is.* The details that follow these clue words and phrases make up the example.

Read the paragraph. Underline the topic sentence. Then circle the example used to prove the point the topic sentence is making.

Some home remedies tell you to do the opposite of what doctors would tell you to do. For example, one home remedy says to put butter on a burn. However, doctors will tell you never to do this. They say that you should run cold water over the burn.

The topic sentence is the first sentence. The three sentences that follow are the example. The sentences support the topic sentence and prove its point.

Read the paragraph. Underline the topic sentence. Then circle the example used to illustrate the main idea.

Jan Brooks applied for a management position in her company. She had been with the company for ten years. She had a high school diploma. She had also taken a six-month course in management. Yet a man who had been with the company for three years was given the position, not Jan. He did not have a high school diploma. He had never taken a course in management. When Jan complained, she was fired. She sued the company for discrimination. She won her suit. Although this type of suit can be hard to prove, many people have taken their cases to court and won.

The last sentence in the paragraph is the topic sentence that states the main idea. The other sentences are supporting details that illustrate the main idea by giving an example.

Check your answers on page 158.

In some paragraphs, supporting details may be organized in more than one way. Some details may be in time order. Some details may show cause and effect. Other details may give an example.

Read the paragraphs and answer the questions.

(1) When you get a sprain, there are certain things you can do. (2) First, elevate the sprained area above your heart. (3) Then put ice on the sprain. (4) The use of ice will result in less swelling. (5) Finally, rest the area for at least 48 hours.

1. Which sentence is the topic sentence?

   _____

2. Write the clue words that tell you this paragraph is mainly organized in time order.

   _____

3. Which two sentences show an example of cause and effect?

   _____

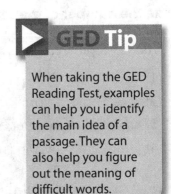

> **GED Tip**
>
> When taking the GED Reading Test, examples can help you identify the main idea of a passage. They can also help you figure out the meaning of difficult words.

At one time, Route 66 was considered one of the most interesting and exciting routes to travel. It began in Chicago and ended in Los Angeles. Along the route, there were all kinds of interesting sights for travelers. You could see the world's largest prairie dog or have lunch in a restaurant shaped like a giant hat.

4. How is the paragraph organized?

   (1) time order
   (2) cause and effect
   (3) compare and contrast
   (4) examples

Check your answers on page 158.

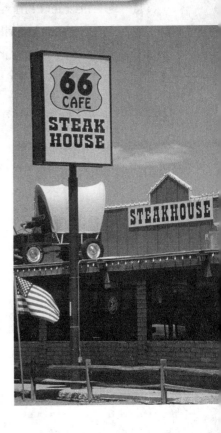

Questions 1–2 are based on the following paragraph.

An insect hovers above a plant in the swamp. The plant has pairs of broad, open leaves. The edges of the leaves have long strands that look like hairs. The insect lands on one of the broad leaves. The other leaf quickly snaps shut over it, trapping the insect. The plant then releases a red fluid. This will dissolve the insect and turn it into food for the plant. The plant is called a Venus' flytrap. It is a carnivorous plant, or a plant that eats insects and small animals.

Circle the number of the correct answer.

1. The example in this paragraph shows that

   (1) the Venus' flytrap is a carnivorous plant.
   (2) the Venus' flytrap does not only catch flies.
   (3) most plants do not eat meat.
   (4) the Venus' flytrap is dangerous to humans.

2. How can you tell that the supporting details give an example?

   (1) The details compare other plants to the Venus' flytrap.
   (2) The details describe the scent of the Venus' flytrap.
   (3) The details explain how the Venus' flytrap catches an insect.
   (4) The details describe where the Venus' flytrap is found.

Question 3 is based on the following paragraph.

The population of the world is growing very quickly. Between the year 1 and the year 1650, the world's population doubled from 250 million to 500 million. From 1650 to 1830, the population doubled again—in less than 200 years. Only 100 years later, there were 2 billion people on earth. Just 40 years later, there were 4 billion!

Circle the number of the correct answer.

3. How is the information in this paragraph organized?

   (1) in time order
   (2) to show a comparison
   (3) to show cause and effect
   (4) both (1) and (2)

Questions 4–5 are based on the following paragraph.

The words *weather* and *climate* have different meanings. *Weather* describes conditions at one time and place. The weather changes every day. One day it can be hot and dry. The next day it can be cool and rainy. *Climate*, on the other hand, is the average weather of a place over a long period of time. For example, we know that winter in New York will be cold. We can expect winter in Florida to be much warmer.

Circle the number of the correct answer.

4. How is the information in this paragraph organized?

   (1) to show cause and effect
   (2) to show a comparison
   (3) to give examples of the main idea
   (4) to show a contrast and give examples

5. What clue word or phrase helped you answer question 4?

   (1) different
   (2) For example
   (3) on the other hand
   (4) all of the above

Check your answers on page 159.

Using a Graphic Organizer

A graphic organizer is a picture that shows how ideas are related. One kind of graphic organizer is a timeline. A timeline shows when things happened. Look at the example.

Important Events in the Space Program

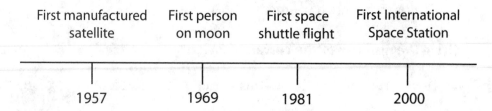
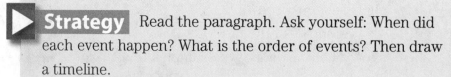

First manufactured satellite	First person on moon	First space shuttle flight	First International Space Station
1957	1969	1981	2000

▶ **Strategy** Read the paragraph. Ask yourself: When did each event happen? What is the order of events? Then draw a timeline.

1. Circle words that tell about time. These words can be days, months, or years.

2. Underline clue words that tell about time order. Some clue words are *first, then, finally,* and *later*.

3. Draw a timeline. Write the dates in order on the timeline. Then write what happened for each date.

Exercise 1: Read the paragraph. Circle dates. Underline clue words about time. On a separate piece of paper, make a timeline.

The United States wanted to thank George Washington. He had been a great leader. He served the country well in times of both war and peace. Congress planned to build a monument for him. In 1783, the first plans were made. Washington heard some of the plans before he died in 1799. In 1848, work began on the monument. Then money ran out and the work had to stop for awhile. Finally, in 1884, the Washington Monument was completed.

A Venn diagram helps you compare and contrast two things. Look at the example. Two kinds of foot coverings—shoes and socks—are compared and contrasted.

Foot Coverings

Shoe   **Both**   **Sock**

hard soles
good for   alking
    outside
protect feet from
    sharp objects

cover feet
available in
    many styles
available in
    many sizes

soft
good for   alking
    inside
prevent blisters

 Strategy Read the paragraph. Find the two things that are compared and contrasted. Ask yourself: How are these things alike? How are they different?

1. Underline clue words and phrases that show things are alike. Some clue words are *too, both,* and *also.*

2. Circle clue words and phrases that show things are different. Some clue words and phrases are *but, different,* and *on the other hand.*

3. In the middle of the Venn diagram, write how the two things are alike. In each oval, write how each thing is different.

Exercise 2: Read the paragraph. Underline clue words about how things are the same. Circle clue words about how they are different. On a separate piece of paper, draw a Venn diagram.

In the city, many people live in apartments. Some people live in houses. In the country, people live in houses too—there aren't really any apartments. In the city, it is often easy to buy what you need at any time of day. But in the country, stores close early. In both places, people like where they live. In the city, the pace is exciting and fast. In the country, on the other hand, the pace is relaxing and slow.

Check your answers on page 159.

Becoming an Active Reader

On the GED Reading Test, you must focus your attention to understand what you are reading. To do this, carefully read each sentence. When you are finished, silently retell the main ideas in that paragraph before you go on to the next one.

 Strategy Try the strategy on the example below. Use these steps.

Step 1 Read the paragraph sentence by sentence.

Step 2 Reread sentences that are hard to understand.

Step 3 Retell all of the important ideas in your own words.

Example

WILL PEOPLE NEAR THE WAAL RIVER BE HELPED?

The Waal River swelled far beyond its banks on Tuesday. Two people were swept away by the flood. Both were later found. One had died. Over 250,000 people have left their homes. Sources say that 140,000 more will leave on Friday. The government has vowed to help bring all who live near the river to higher ground.

Which is the best retelling of the paragraph?

(1) Some people have had to leave their homes. One person died.

(2) The river flooded. The government is helping everyone who lives near the river.

(3) The Waal River flooded. One person died. Many people are being asked to leave their homes. The government is helping them.

(4) Two people were swept away. One lived and one died.

In Step 1 you read the paragraph. In Step 2 you reread sentences that were hard to understand. In Step 3 you retold the main ideas and chose the answer that was closest to your retelling. The correct answer is (3). This answer includes all the important ideas. Choices (1), (2), and (4) only retell a couple of ideas.

Practice the strategy. Use the steps you learned. Answer the questions.

WHAT HAPPENED TO THE CALIFORNIA CONDOR?

In 1987, the last few wild California condors were caught. These birds joined others that lived in zoos or shelters. Scientists hoped that the condors would have chicks. The young birds would be raised and then set free into the wild. The U.S. Fish & Wildlife Service thought that these steps would help the birds survive.

The condors did have chicks. Scientists did not want the chicks to bond with humans. To keep the chicks wild, many were raised using puppets that looked like condors. Some were raised by their real condor parents.

Ninety-nine California condors have been set free and now live in the wild. Even more live in programs that protect and care for them. Some of these protected birds will also be set free.

1. Retell the main point of the second paragraph in your own words.

_____

_____

_____

2. Which of the following is the best retelling of the last paragraph?

(1) Wild California condors were caught. Their chicks hatched. Some were set free and others are being cared for.

(2) Ninety-nine California condors live in the wild. Others live in programs that will take care of them until they are freed.

(3) Chicks that were hatched were raised by their parents or puppets.

(4) Scientists wanted the condor chicks to stay wild. Some were raised by people using puppets, and others were raised by their parents.

Check your answers on page 159.

Read each paragraph and question carefully. Circle the number of the correct answer.

Questions 1–3 are based on the following paragraph.

WHAT'S SPECIAL ABOUT THE NEW WATER PARK?

The new water park is similar to River Park, but it has more water slides. Two slides are indoors. This means the park can stay open year-round, unlike River Park. River Park closes each fall. The new arcade area is also larger than River Park's. River Park plans to update its park. River Park doesn't want to lose business to the new water park.

1. In what ways are the new water park and River Park alike?

   (1) Both are open year-round.

   (2) Both close in the fall.

   (3) Both have the same number of slides.

   (4) Both have water slides and an arcade area.

2. Which clue words show how the paragraph is organized?

   (1) unlike

   (2) also

   (3) similar

   (4) all of the above

3. What is the effect of the new park on River Park?

   (1) River Park will close for good.

   (2) River Park will be updated.

   (3) River Park is moving.

   (4) River Park is adding an arcade area.

Questions 4–6 are based on the following paragraph.

> ## HOW DO YOU PREPARE TO TAKE UP A NEW SPORT?
>
> You've decided you want to take up a new sport. What should you do? First, be sure that you are healthy. You don't want to make any physical problems worse. Next, find out what you need to buy. You might need shoes or safety equipment. Finally, you might want to take a class about the sport to get started. Whatever you do, make sure you have fun!

4. How is the paragraph organized?

   (1) by showing what happens and why

   (2) by showing likenesses and differences

   (3) by giving steps that you should follow

   (4) by giving examples

5. What types of clues tell you how the paragraph is organized?

   (1) comparing and contrasting

   (2) cause and effect

   (3) examples

   (4) time order

6. What could result from not being healthy?

   (1) You may need extra safety equipment.

   (2) You may need a class.

   (3) Your physical problems might get worse.

   (4) You might not know what to buy.

HOW DID DANIEL BOONE FEEL ABOUT HIS WIFE?

There are some famous folktales about American pioneers. One is about how Daniel Boone met his wife, Rebecca. One day, Daniel was hunting. He thought he saw a deer in the brush and ran after it. He ended up at a neighbor's home. A young woman named Rebecca was there. She was breathless from running. Daniel had been running after her, not a deer. The story is that Daniel fell in love at that instant. He loved Rebecca all his life.

7. How does the author show how Daniel felt about his wife?

   (1) by telling a story about how Daniel fell in love

   (2) by explaining the effects of Daniel falling in love

   (3) by comparing Daniel before and after he fell in love

   (4) by telling the steps that led to Daniel falling in love

8. Which sentence indicates that this is an example of a folktale?

   (1) One is about how Daniel Boone met his wife, Rebecca.

   (2) He ended up at a neighbor's home.

   (3) A young woman named Rebecca was there.

   (4) The story is that Daniel fell in love at that instant.

Check your answers on page 160.

Unit 3 Skill Check-Up Chart

Check your answers. In the first column, circle the numbers of any questions that you missed. Then look across the rows to see the skills you need to review and the pages where you can find each skill.

Question	Skill	Page
4, 5	Showing Time Order	66–69
1, 2	Comparing and Contrasting	70–73
3, 6	Showing Cause and Effect	74–77
7, 8	Giving Examples	78–81

Unit 4   Interpreting What You Read

In this unit you will learn about

- **making inferences**
- **drawing conclusions**
- **identifying fact and opinion**
- **detecting bias**

fact

imply

opinion

bias

When you read, you think about the facts and details that are presented and what they mean. You also "read between the lines." This means you figure out some information on your own. Suppose you read a story about a woman who wants to visit a famous city to see the White House. You would be able to figure out that she wants to visit Washington, D.C.

When do you read between the lines to figure out information in your daily life?

_____

_____

In this unit you will learn how to figure out information on your own. You will also learn how to tell opinions from facts.

Write one fact about your day so far. Then write your opinion about how the day is going.

_____

_____

_____

infer
figure out from given information

imply
does not directly state; suggest

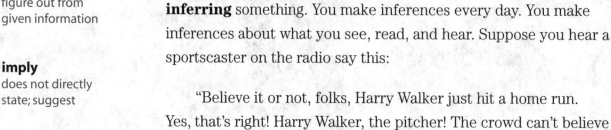

When you figure out something on your own, you are **inferring** something. You make inferences every day. You make inferences about what you see, read, and hear. Suppose you hear a sportscaster on the radio say this:

"Believe it or not, folks, Harry Walker just hit a home run. Yes, that's right! Harry Walker, the pitcher! The crowd can't believe it either!"

The sportscaster tells you a fact—Harry Walker hit a home run. But the sportscaster **implies**, or suggests, something more. She says, "Believe it or not." She repeats Harry's name as if she is surprised. She says, "The crowd can't believe it either." From these clues, you can infer that Harry Walker doesn't usually hit home runs. However, the sportscaster never directly states that information.

Read the paragraph. Then answer the questions.

Pat checked her recipe as she walked through the grocery store. She had all the ingredients to make the cake. All she needed was powdered sugar for the frosting and some candles. Pat had just enough time to make the cake and wrap the presents before Terri came home from school.

1. What can you infer about Terri?

   _____

2. What clues helped you infer this?

   _____

   _____

   _____

Check your answers on page 160.

When you read, you make inferences based on the information that is provided. You read between the lines. You understand things that aren't directly stated.

Inferences are not guesses. Inferences are based on the information given. Your inference must be supported by details from your reading. These details are **evidence**. They prove that your inference is correct.

evidence
information that proves something is true

Read the paragraph. Then answer the questions.

> Mrs. Connelly rested her head on the back of the chair in her living room. She weakly lifted her hand and wiped her forehead. Her ruby ring slipped down her thin finger. The large jewel shone in the light. A man wearing a white coat sat beside her. He took her hand and pressed two fingers to the inside of her wrist as he checked his watch. "How are you feeling today, Mrs. Connelly?" he asked.

1. Who is the man speaking to Mrs. Connelly?

   _____

2. What evidence supports your answer?

   _____

   _____

As you read this paragraph, you can figure out that it tells about a doctor's visit. Details suggest that Mrs. Connelly is ill. They also hint at her status, or position in life.

Answer the question.

3. What can you infer about whether Mrs. Connelly is rich or poor?

   _____

   _____

Check your answers on page 160.

> **GED Tip**
>
> The answer to a question on the GED Reading Test may not be directly stated in the passage. Look for information that can be inferred.

Practice

Questions 1–2 are based on the following paragraph.

> Jackie Lynch gets up at 6:00 every morning. She studies her nursing books before she leaves for her job at Quick Mart each day. Jackie attends classes three nights a week. On weekends, she helps at a free health clinic. This has been Jackie's routine for two years.

Write your answers to the questions below.

1. What can you infer that Jackie wants to be?

   _____

2. What can you infer about the kind of worker Jackie is?

   _____

   _____

Questions 3–4 are based on the following paragraph.

> Tom ran a hand through his gray hair and yawned. He took off his reading glasses and reached for his cane. He slowly pushed himself out of the chair. Every day it was harder for Tom to get up. It was also getting harder to straighten his back.

Circle the number of the correct answer.

3. You can infer that Tom is

   (1) young.
   (2) old.
   (3) poor.
   (4) healthy.

4. You can also infer that Tom

   (1) was enjoying his book.
   (2) has trouble sleeping.
   (3) has trouble walking.
   (4) is going to have lunch.

Questions 5–6 are based on the following ad.

TRY GRIME OUT!
Bring New Life to Your Old Carburetor!

Does your ignition grind on and on before your car finally starts? Does your car stall? Is it using more gas than it should? Then try GRIME OUT! GRIME OUT cleans out carburetors and fuel lines by attacking dirt and gummy buildup. After using just one bottle of GRIME OUT, your car will run smoother than ever!

Circle the number of the correct answer.

5. From this ad, you can infer that if your car is hard to start, then

    (1) your carburetor may be dirty.

    (2) your fuel line may have gummy buildup.

    (3) you should try a different brand of gas.

    (4) both (1) and (2)

6. You can also infer that

    (1) Grime Out will harm your fuel system.

    (2) Grime Out takes a long time to work.

    (3) Grime Out takes very little time to work.

    (4) Grime Out will not work at all.

Check your answers on page 160.

draw a conclusion
figure out something based on facts, inferences, and what you already know about a subject

When you **draw a conclusion**, you first look at the information you have. You think about the details that give you information, and figure out what you can infer from those details. Next, you combine this information with what you already know about the subject from your own life. Now you are ready to draw a conclusion.

Read the paragraph. Then draw a conclusion about Billy.

> Billy came quacking out of the barn and waddled toward the pond. When he got to the edge, he flapped his wings loudly and hopped into the water.

What can you conclude about Billy?

_____

To draw a conclusion, first look at the facts and inferences.

- **Facts**—Billy quacks; Billy waddles toward the pond and hops into the water; Billy has wings.
- **Inference**—Billy likes water.

Now think about what you already know. If Billy quacks, waddles, has wings, and likes water, he must be a duck.

Read the paragraph.

> There are nine planets in our solar system. They all travel around the sun. The planets listed in order are Mercury, Venus, Earth, Mars, Jupiter, Saturn, Uranus, Neptune, and Pluto. Mercury is closest to the sun. Venus is next, and so on. The closer a planet is to the sun, the hotter that planet is. The temperature on Mercury can reach 625°F. But Mars, which is farther from the sun, has temperatures as low as -191°F.

Look at the details provided in the paragraph on page 94.

- The planets are listed in order from closest to farthest from the sun.

- The temperature on each planet depends on how far away from the sun it is.

- Mercury is closest to the sun and has temperatures as high 625°F.

- Mars is farther from the sun and has temperatures as low as -191°F.

Write the answer to the question below.

1. What can you conclude about the temperature on Pluto?

_____

_____

Read this paragraph. Then answer the question.

> People once thought that there was life on Mars. Others believed that there really was a "man in the moon." Now we know more about our solar system. We know that only one planet in our solar system can support human life.

2. You can conclude that the only planet in our solar system that can support human life must be

_____

To draw a conclusion, ask yourself these questions:

- What do I know after reading the paragraph?
- What can I add from my own experience?
- What can I conclude?

Check your answers on page 161.

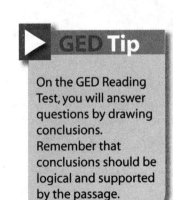

> **GED Tip**
>
> On the GED Reading Test, you will answer questions by drawing conclusions. Remember that conclusions should be logical and supported by the passage.

Question 1–2 are based on the following paragraph.

> Mr. and Mrs. Martin live in a grand old home. Every night at 5:00, they eat their dinner in the large dining room. After dinner, Mr. Martin reads his paper. Mrs. Martin reads her book. At 7:00, they watch TV. At 9:00 sharp, they both go to bed.

Write your answers to the questions below.

1. What can you conclude about the Martins' daily life?

   _____

   _____

2. What information supports your conclusion?

   _____

Question 3 is based on the following paragraph.

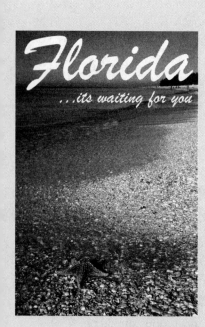

> Have the winter blues got you down? Are you tired of cold temperatures and icy sidewalks? It may be winter where you live, but things are heating up in Florida! Book your trip today while airfares are low. Take a trip to Florida—it's more reasonably priced than you think.

Circle the number of the correct answer.

3. From the paragraph, you can conclude that
   (1) it's cold and snowy in Florida.
   (2) it's warm and pleasant in Florida.
   (3) it's expensive to travel to Florida.
   (4) it's best to travel to Florida once winter is over.

Questions 4–6 are based on the following passage.

The U.S. Department of Agriculture makes the following recommendations about diet.

- Eat a variety of foods. You need vitamins, minerals, proteins, carbohydrates, and fat. No single food can give you all these things.

- Choose foods that are low in total fat, saturated fat, and cholesterol. Too much fat and cholesterol can lead to heart disease and other health problems.

- Eat lots of vegetables, fruits, and grains. Every day, eat at least three servings of vegetables, two servings of fruit, and six servings of grains.

Circle the number of the correct answer.

4. From this passage, you can conclude that

  (1) a balanced diet includes many different foods.
  (2) a diet that includes any fat is bad for you.
  (3) you should eat only fruits and vegetables.
  (4) grains are the best food for you to eat.

5. From the information in the passage, you can conclude that

  (1) you should eat the same foods every day.
  (2) you should eat more than one serving of many kinds of foods each day.
  (3) you should avoid having too many servings of grains.
  (4) too many servings of vegetables can lead to heart disease.

6. From the passage, you can conclude that

  (1) heart problems are caused by not getting enough fat.
  (2) all foods have vitamins.
  (3) some foods are better for you than others.
  (4) vegetables are better for you than grains.

Check your answers on page 161.

Imagine that you are having breakfast. As you pour a glass of juice, you read these two statements on the side of the carton.

> A 6-ounce glass of Top of the Morning Fruit Juice has only 120 calories and provides 100 percent of the vitamin C you need each day.

> Top of the Morning is the best tasting juice in the world!

Write your answer to the question below.

Which statement would you believe? Why?

_____

_____

_____

fact
something that is true or can be proved

You probably chose the first statement. It tells **facts** about the number of calories and how much vitamin C a glass of juice contains. This statement can be proved.

opinion
what a person thinks, believes, or feels about something

The second statement does not tell facts. It gives an **opinion**. An opinion cannot be proved. Not everyone would agree that this brand is the best tasting juice in the world.

How can you tell if a statement is an opinion? Look for these word clues that signal what someone thinks or believes: *seems, think, believe, feel, appears,* and *in my opinion.*

If there are no clues, ask yourself the following questions.

■ Can this statement be proved?

■ Would everyone agree that this is true?

If the answer to either question is *no,* the statement is an opinion.

Read these two paragraphs. Underline clues that signal an opinion. Then circle the letter of the correct answer.

> More and more states have passed laws to create a smoke-free workplace. These laws state that an employer must provide nonsmokers with a work area where no smoking is allowed. Some states have banned smoking in all public places.

> Many states have already passed laws that give nonsmokers the right to have a smoke-free place to work. Why doesn't our state have laws that do that? I think it's awful that I have to breathe smoke all day. In my opinion, smoking should be illegal in all public places. Until that happens, I should at least have a healthy place to work.

1. Which paragraph contains mostly opinions?

   (a) the first paragraph
   (b) the second paragraph

2. Which paragraph contains mostly facts?

   (a) the first paragraph
   (b) the second paragraph

Both paragraphs are about laws that ban or limit smoking. But the paragraphs are very different. The first paragraph tells facts about smoking laws. This information can be proved. You can check the laws to see if the statements are true.

The second paragraph gives opinions about the laws. This paragraph begins with a fact, but the other sentences tell how the writer feels about this fact. These sentences are opinions. They cannot be proved.

GED Tip

On the GED Reading Test, you answer questions about an author's opinion. Look for clue words and phrases and for information that cannot be proven in order to find the author's opinions.

Check your answers on page 162.

Questions 1–2 are based on the following newspaper articles.

Article 1

Dining Out

Down South, a new restaurant at 411 Pine Street, is supposed to serve traditional southern food. The fried catfish we ate was tender and crisp. The fried chicken and cornbread were both delicious. But the cooking wasn't southern. The catfish was coated with flour. The chicken was fried in batter. And why do people in the North insist on putting sugar in cornbread? This just isn't done in the South.

Article 2

What's Cooking?

Down South is a new restaurant at 411 Pine Street that serves southern foods. For the main course, there is fried catfish, fried chicken, or chicken-fried steak. Side dishes are turnip greens, blackeyed peas, and cornbread. The desserts include pecan pie and sweet potato pie. There's also boiled custard. The restaurant is open every day for lunch and dinner. Meals range in price from $6.95 to $14.95.

Circle the number of the correct answer.

1. What opinion is given in article 1 about the food at Down South?

    (1) It's awful.

    (2) It's good but not southern.

    (3) It's excellent.

    (4) The writer doesn't give an opinion.

2. What opinion is given in article 2 about the food at Down South?

    (1) It's great.

    (2) It's awful.

    (3) It's too expensive.

    (4) The writer doesn't give an opinion.

Questions 3–5 are based on the following paragraph.

Less than 55 percent of U.S. citizens vote in presidential elections. Even fewer citizens vote in local elections. In my opinion, there should be a law that requires people to vote in every election. People who do not vote would not be able to get a passport. They would not be allowed to travel to other countries. If people were forced to vote, I think it would help our country. Our system of democracy would be stronger. Those who win an election would truly be chosen by the people they serve.

Circle the number of the correct answer.

3. What is the writer's purpose in writing this paragraph?

   (1) The writer wants to tell people how to get a passport.
   (2) The writer wants to tell people about voting laws.
   (3) The writer wants a law that requires people to vote.
   (4) The writer wants to stop people from traveling outside the country.

4. What fact does the writer use to support his or her opinion?

   (1) Less than 55 percent of U.S. citizens vote in presidential elections.
   (2) A passport is needed to travel out of the country.
   (3) A passport is needed to vote in presidential elections.
   (4) Our democratic system would be stronger if more people voted.

5. Which clue word or phrase shows you that the writer is expressing an opinion?

   (1) think
   (2) In my opinion
   (3) believe
   (4) both (1) and (2)

Check your answers on page 162.

Lesson 15   Detecting Bias

bias
strong feeling for or against something

influence
affect the way a person thinks

loaded word
a word that creates an emotional response

Writers may show **bias**. They let the reader know if they feel strongly for or against something. You can find this bias by thinking about words the writer uses. Certain words are meant to get the reader to do something or to feel a certain way. These words are meant to **influence** the reader.

Read the following sentence.

■ The man was tall and trim.

How do you picture this person? You may picture someone whose height is above average and who has an athletic body.

Read the following sentence.

■ The man was tall and thin.

Now you may picture someone who is tall but weighs less than average.

Read the following sentence.

■ The man was tall and skinny.

Now the person seems underweight. You might even think the person is not healthy.

The words *trim, thin,* and *skinny* mean nearly the same thing. However, each word makes us feel a different way. Writers are aware of the feelings behind words. They sometimes use **loaded words** to get their readers to do something or feel a certain way. Once you understand why writers use certain words and how those words are supposed to make you feel, you can decide for yourself whether you agree or disagree with the writer.

Read the following book reviews.

Review 1:

Miguel Edwards has done it again! His new book, *Panning for Gold*, is bound to be a classic. His characters are unforgettable. Edwards keeps the reader in suspense right up to his surprise ending. Edwards is a talented writer who will likely win awards for this book and gain many new fans.

Review 2:

Miguel Edwards shows greed struggling with friendship in his new book, *Panning for Gold*. The main character, Bruce Goldsmith, is faced with a problem. Goldsmith must choose between a dear friend and a large amount of money. What happens next may shock the reader.

In the first review, the writer's opinion of the book is clear. The review is filled with praise. The author "has done it again." The book "is bound to be a classic." The author is "talented." The characters are not just interesting, they are "unforgettable." This review shows bias. The writer tries to get readers to do something—read *Panning for Gold*.

In the second review, the writer's opinion of the book is not known. The words in this review are **neutral**. They don't touch our emotions. They don't try to convince us of something. This writer does not show bias.

neutral
showing no feeling for or against something

Read the following sentences from different reviews. Write *B* for biased or *N* for neutral on each line.

_____ **1.** Once again, Hugo's film is among the very best.

_____ **2.** The two enemies are asked to work together.

_____ **3.** This book won the National Book Award.

_____ **4.** The amazing ending will bring you to your feet!

Check your answers on page 162.

GED Tip

When you read a passage on the GED Reading Test, try to recognize the author's bias. This will help you to understand the author's opinions.

Questions 1–3 are based on the following report.

Nearly sixty parents filed into the large meeting room. They did not want their children's school to close. The head of the school board rose to speak. He spoke to people as if they were his friends. He had probably never spoken to them before in his life. His folded suit coat was over the back of his chair. Then he rolled up his shirtsleeves to look like a man of the people. He smiled as if he cared about the people in the room, but his eyes were cold. Then he stepped to the head of the table and got ready to speak.

Write your answers to the questions.

1. What is the writer's opinion of the head of the school board?

   _____

   _____

   _____

2. Write an example from the paragraph that shows how the writer feels about the head of the school board.

   _____

   _____

   _____

3. Does the writer think that the head of the school board cares about the people in the room and their concerns? Why or why not?

   _____

   _____

   _____

   _____

Questions 4–6 are based on the following articles.

Article 1:

Kate Reeves, a professor who was fired from State University, is suing her former employer. She says she was fired because she refused to give six football players a passing grade. Athletes who receive a failing grade are not allowed to participate in sports. But the university let them play and fired Reeves instead.

Article 2:

Kate Reeves is suing State University. The gruff former professor complains bitterly that she should not have been fired. She claims she was let go when she would not give six football players a passing grade that they did not deserve. Officials at the university say that the emotional Reeves is just not a good teacher. The students would have passed if she had done her job.

Circle the number of the correct answer.

4. How are the two articles different?

   (1) One is about the school, and one is about Kate Reeves.

   (2) Both are about football players and their grades.

   (3) One is biased against Kate Reeves, and one is not.

   (4) One talks about the lawsuit, and the other does not.

5. Which of the following is a loaded word?

   (1) gruff

   (2) suing

   (3) emotional

   (4) both (1) and (3)

6. What does the writer of article 2 want you to think of Kate Reeves?

   (1) She is a good teacher who was fired unfairly.

   (2) She was fired because she disliked athletes.

   (3) She tried hard to be cooperative with school officials.

   (4) She was a bad teacher who was treated fairly.

Check your answers on page 162.

Interpreting Ideas

When you make inferences, you read between the lines. You figure out information that is not directly stated. You also use what you know to draw conclusions. Making inferences and drawing conclusions help you to have a more complete understanding of what you read.

 Strategy Read the paragraph. Ask yourself: What clues will I use to help me understand the meaning of any unfamiliar words?

1. Look at the facts and details in the paragraph.

2. Ask yourself: What can I infer from reading between the lines?

3. Ask yourself: What can I conclude from what I have read?

Exercise 1: Read the paragraph. Then answer the questions.

> Everyone in the Lopez family is learning English. They need to speak English at school and at their jobs. Their apartment is small, and it is neat and clean. The walls need some painting, and the screen door wobbles a bit. The sofa is worn, and there is only a small television set. From the streets below, you can hear the sounds of the cars and buses.

1. Where can you infer that the family's apartment is found?

   (a) in the city

   (b) in the country

2. What clues in the paragraph help you to infer this?

   _____

3. Write one thing that you can conclude about the Lopez family.

   _____

Knowing how to tell a fact from an opinion will help you as you read. You can decide if something is true or if someone is trying to get you to do or believe something.

 Strategy Read the paragraph. Ask yourself: Which statements can be proved? Which statements tell what someone thinks or feels?

1. Sometimes a clue word or phrase signals an opinion. Some of these clue words and phrases are *think, believe,* and *in my opinion.*

2. Look for loaded words. These words are used to convince you to believe what the writer wants you to believe.

Exercise 2: Read the paragraph. Then answer the questions.

I believe that the seat belt laws in our state are not harsh enough. Those careless people who drive without wearing seat belts should be forced to give up their driver's licenses. If they do not know the rules of the road, why are they driving? What other laws do they ignore? Their licenses should be returned only if they complete a safe-driving class.

1. What clue word tells you that the writer is giving an opinion?

_____

2. How does the writer want you to feel about people who drive without wearing seat belts?

_____

_____

3. Which word in the second sentence is a loaded word?

_____

Check your answers on page 163.

Choosing the Right Answer

On the GED Reading Test, you answer multiple-choice questions. It may seem difficult to choose the right answer, but there are ways to help you figure out which answer is correct.

 Strategy Try this strategy with the following example. Use these steps.

Step 1 Read the question. Be sure you know what it is asking.

Step 2 Read each answer choice. Cross out any that you know are wrong.

Step 3 Check the information in the passage.

Step 4 Choose the best remaining answer.

WHAT ARE THE PARTS OF A SPIDER'S BODY?

All spiders have two body parts. The spider's head is part of the cephalothorax, which is the first part of the spider's body. All eight of a spider's legs are attached to this part. The second part of the spider's body is the abdomen. The heart and lungs are found here.

What is found in or on the abdomen of the spider's body?

(1) four of the spider's legs

(2) eight of the spider's legs

(3) the head

(4) the heart and lungs

In Step 1 you read the question. In Step 2 you read all of the answer choices and crossed out the ones that you knew were wrong. In Step 3 you checked the passage. Choice (1) is incorrect because all of the legs are attached to the cephalothorax. Choice (2) may seem correct because all of a spider's legs are attached to one part of the body, but looking back at the passage shows they are attached to the cephalothorax. Choice (3) is incorrect because the head is part of the cephalothorax. In Step 4 you chose the best remaining answer. The correct answer is (4).

Practice the strategy. Use the steps you have learned. Circle the number of the correct answer.

HOW FAST WAS THE PONY EXPRESS?

The Pony Express was the first express mail service. In 1860, mail was carried by stagecoach. It took three weeks for mail from the East to reach the West. Some businessmen thought of a way to give faster service. They created the Pony Express. Riders carried the mail on horseback from Missouri to California in about ten days.

1. Why was the Pony Express created?

   (1) to provide mail service to California
   (2) to provide faster mail service to California
   (3) to provide mail service to the Midwest
   (4) to try out new ways to deliver the mail

SHOULD THERE BE A TSUNAMI WARNING SYSTEM?

A tsunami hit Indian Ocean coastlines in late 2004. A tsunami is a huge wave caused by an earthquake under the ocean floor. In the 2004 tsunami, the wave was 33 feet tall. In an instant, people were swept out to sea. Homes and boats were flooded. The death toll climbed by the hour. In the end, hundreds of thousands of people lost their lives. Many people asked whether a warning system should have been in place.

2. What can happen as a result of a tsunami?

   (1) an earthquake can occur
   (2) the ocean floor can be damaged
   (3) people can be swept out to sea
   (4) islands are formed

Check your answers on page 163.

GED Test Practice

Read each paragraph and question carefully. Circle the number of the correct answer.

Questions 1–3 are based on the following paragraph.

WHAT IS THE NEW TELEVISION PROGRAM ABOUT?

"Here Today, Gone Tomorrow" is a new TV drama about wandering artist Monroe Cobb. As he arrives in each new city, Cobb meets people and gets involved in their lives. He is known for saying, "I paint them as I see them." Each show ends with a view of Cobb's canvas.

1. What inference can be made about Cobb's paintings?
   (1) He paints mainly in reds and greens.
   (2) He paints cheerful scenes.
   (3) He paints people.
   (4) He paints special buildings and statues.

2. What conclusion can be drawn about the new TV program?
   (1) It will show a new way of looking at people's lives.
   (2) It will focus on how much an artist can earn.
   (3) It will focus on a new mystery every week.
   (4) It will show the problems artists face in their work.

3. What inference can be made from the title of the show?
   (1) Cobb will only meet people in the arts.
   (2) Cobb never stays long in one community.
   (3) Cobb will marry and travel with his wife.
   (4) Cobb is a heartless person.

Questions 4–6 are based on the following passage.

WHAT ARE GOOD MANNERS?

At one time it was considered impolite for a woman to smoke in public. Now this rule applies to both men and women. At one time men opened doors for women. Today, it is polite for whoever gets to the door first, male or female, to open it.

Manners have always been a way to show concern for others. I believe that children today are not taught these valuable habits. They selfishly grab the best for themselves. In school, they push to the front of the line. In stores, they demand the most expensive toys. Parents act as if their children deserve the best of everything.

4. What conclusion can you draw from the first paragraph?

   (1) Women should be allowed to smoke as much as men.

   (2) Men should hold doors for women.

   (3) Being polite is not important.

   (4) Manners are always changing.

5. What words in paragraph two show that the writer is expressing an opinion?

   (1) believe

   (2) school

   (3) demand

   (4) deserve

6. Which of the following sentences shows the writer's bias?

   (1) Manners have always been a way to show concern for others.

   (2) They selfishly grab the best for themselves.

   (3) Now this rule applies to both men and women.

   (4) At one time men opened doors for women.

Questions 7–8 are based on the following paragraph.

> ## DOES DRAKE SUCCEED IN HER NEW MOVIE?
>
> *The Great Jewel Caper,* starring Rose Drake, opens this weekend. Drake hasn't made a film in three years, when she was unforgettable in the powerful movie *Four Hundred Roses.* In her new movie, Drake's flawless performance stirs the audience. They weep for her character, the doomed wife.

7. Which of these shows the writer's bias about *The Great Jewel Caper*?

   (1) Drake's performance was "flawless."
   (2) Drake's earlier movie was "powerful."
   (3) Drake's character is a "doomed wife."
   (4) Drake hasn't "made a film in three years."

8. Which of the following is a fact?

   (1) Drake was unforgettable in *Four Hundred Roses.*
   (2) Drake's flawless performance stirs the audience.
   (3) *Four Hundred Roses* was a powerful movie.
   (4) *The Great Jewel Caper* opens this weekend.

Check your answers on page 164.

Unit 4 Skill Check-Up Chart

Check your answers. In the first column circle the numbers of any questions that you have missed. Then look across the rows to see the skill you need to review and the pages where you can find each skill.

Question	Skill	Page
1, 3	Making Inferences	90–93
2, 4	Drawing Conclusions	94–97
5, 8	Identifying Fact and Opinion	98–101
6, 7	Detecting Bias	102–105

Unit 5 · Understanding Fiction and Poetry

plot

stanza

theme

mood

In this unit you will learn about

- character and setting
- plot and conflict
- theme and mood
- imagery in poetry

Novels and short stories are works of fiction. Think about a story you like. What do you like about it? The action? The characters? Or do you like the story's message?

What is your favorite story, and why do you like it?

_____

_____

Character, setting, plot, mood, and theme are all important elements of fiction. Poetry also contains its own important elements. Think about a poem or song that has a special meaning for you.

What comes to mind when you think about the poem or song?

_____

_____

Lesson 16   Understanding Character and Setting

characters
the people in a story

main character
the central character
in a story

traits
a person's qualities

Almost every story you read has **characters**. As you read, pay attention to details the writer uses to describe characters. Details let you know what the characters look like and why they act as they do.

Suppose you are reading a story about a woman. She is the **main character** in the story. As you read, you learn how she acts in certain situations. You read what other characters say about her and how they treat her. All these details help you to see some of her **traits**, or qualities. These traits help you get to know the character.

Read the paragraph. Then answer the questions.

I looked at Aunt Tiger, who was unusually quiet. She was very different from Mother, who was tall, slender, and elegant. Aunt Tiger was stocky and round. She didn't go quietly about her duties, always trying to make the best of everything, as Mother did. She spoke her mind, and often complained bitterly. I thought it refreshing to hear her complain, for she so often said what I was feeling.

From *Year of Impossible Goodbyes*,
by Sook Nyul Choi

1. What does Aunt Tiger look like?

_____

_____

2. How does Aunt Tiger usually act?

_____

_____

Check your answers on page 164.

The **setting** describes where and when the story takes place. Suppose a story begins with the sentence "It was a steaming hot night in Atlanta." This one sentence directly gives you several details about the setting. The story takes place at night, in Atlanta. The sentence also gives you details indirectly. Because the night is "steaming hot," the setting is probably summer.

The next sentence tells you more of the story: "As we sat in Rob's yard and listened to ghost stories, the fire from the grill flared up." This further describes the setting. The story takes place outside, in Rob's yard. If the author then describes Rob's yard, those details also become part of the setting.

When you read, look for details that tell you where the characters are and when the events take place. Understanding the setting will help you to better understand the story.

setting
where and when events
in a story take place

Read the paragraph. Then answer the questions.

> The snow-dusted hill on which the brothers stood stretched down toward the great wall that surrounded Seoul. The road that wound around the base of the hill led to one of the city's nine enormous gates. Beyond the wall Young-sup could see hundreds of rooftops, huddled together and crouched low to the ground, as if bowing to the palace at the center of the city. The grand tiled roofs of the royal palace stood out in graceful curved splendor[1]. No other structure[2] was permitted to rise higher.
>
> [1] beauty
> [2] building
>
> From *The Kite Fighters*, by Linda Sue Park

1. Near what city does the story take place?

_____

2. Where are the brothers standing?

_____

GED Tip

When you read a passage on the GED Reading Test, look for details that describe the characters and the setting.

Check your answers on page 164.

Practice

> The prairie was like a giant plate, stretching all the way to the sky at the edges. And we were like two tiny peas left over from dinner, Lester and me. We couldn't even see the soddy[1] from out there—just nothing, nothing in a big circle all around us. We still had Cap then, and he stood very still, shaking his harness now and again while we did our work, throwing cow chips into the back of the wagon, me singing all the while.
>
> "Buffalo chips, buffalo chips, won't you marry me? Oh, come on out, buffalo chips, and dance all night by the sea."
>
> Lester smiled and kept up a complicated clicking sound with his tongue and throat.
>
> "Come on, Lester," I told him. "Sing! Nobody can hear ya out here."
>
> [1] house built from sod, or earth   From *Prairie Songs*, by Pam Conrad

Answer the questions.

1. One character in the passage is the narrator. Who is the other human character?

   _____

2. Where does this story take place?

   _____

Circle the letter of the correct answer.

3. What does the narrator's song tell you about her personality?

   (a) She is serious about her work.

   (b) She has a good sense of humor.

Questions 4–5 are based on the following passage.

They both sat down hesitantly. The man folded his arms and looked rather sullen, the woman stared at Victor's walrus mustache.

"Oh, that's just for camouflage[1]," he explained, pulling the mustache from his lip. "Quite a necessity in my line of work. Well, what can I do for you? Anything lost or stolen, any pet run away?"

Without saying a word, the woman reached into her bag. She had ash-blonde hair and a pointed nose. Her mouth didn't look as if smiling was its favorite activity. The man was a giant, at least two full heads taller than Victor. His nose was peeling from sunburn and his eyes were small and dull. Doesn't look like he can take a joke either, Victor thought, as he committed the two faces to memory. He could never remember a phone number, but he never forgot a face.

[1] disguise   From *The Thief Lord*, by Cornelia Funke

Circle the number of the correct answer.

4. Which of these sentences describes the woman in the story?

   (1) She's tall and sunburned.
   (2) She has dark hair and brown eyes.
   (3) She has ash-blonde hair and doesn't smile.
   (4) She had folded arms and dull eyes.

5. What can you guess about the man from the way he acts in the first paragraph?

   (1) He is not in a good mood.
   (2) He knows Victor.
   (3) He is eager to talk with Victor.
   (4) He is happy Victor is helping.

Check your answers on page 165.

plot
a series of actions or events; what happens in a story

event
something that happens, especially something exciting, unusual, or interesting

You have read about two important story elements, character and setting. Another important story element is **plot**. The plot tells what happens in a story through a series of **events**, or actions. One way to understand the plot of a story is to think about the actions that happen.

Read the passage. Complete the chart with the missing actions.

> Suddenly, the driver of an engine pulled his horses to a stop and the crew jumped down. One man put a wrench to the hydrant while two others twisted a hose onto the tank. With a rallying cry, another ran to the end of the hose and lifted the shiny brass nozzle. Seconds passed. The man with the wrench threw his weight into opening the valve. Finally he dropped his hands.
>
> "She's empty here, too, lads. God help us!"
>
> From *Earthquake at Dawn*, by Kristiana Gregory

Actions in the Story	
Action 1	The driver of an engine stopped his horses, and the crew jumped down.
Action 2	
Action 3	A man ran to the end of the hose and lifted the nozzle.
Action 4	
Action 5	The man who opened the valve of the hydrant said it was dry, too.

Check your answers on page 165.

The plot of a story is often based on a **conflict**, or problem. A conflict happens when there is a struggle between two or more people or things. The word *conflict* may bring to mind an argument or a military battle. However, there are many kinds of conflict.

conflict
a struggle between two opposing forces

Suppose you read a story in which a football player uses steroids, even though their use is forbidden. Another player finds out. He threatens to tell the team owners about what he knows. The conflict is between the two athletes.

The conflict in a story is usually presented early. As you read, more details about the conflict are revealed. Then the characters either solve the problem, or the situation changes. The conflict comes to an end.

Read the passage. Then answer the questions.

> *This can't be happening.* Mark edged toward the nearest tree. The instant he moved, the beast spotted him. It pawed the ground with its large hooves and lowered its massive head to attack.
>
> There was no time to think. Mark jumped for the closest branch and swung up into the tree just as the sharp tusks rushed underneath him. The animal stopped and sniffed the air again. Unable to locate its victim, the creature snorted and ambled[1] off into the red forest.

[1] walked   From *The Transall Saga*, by Gary Paulsen

GED Tip

On the GED Reading Test, focus on the important events in a passage. This will help you identify a conflict and its solution.

1. In the passage, who is the conflict between?

    _____

2. How does Mark solve the problem?

    _____

Check your answers on page 165.

Questions 1–2 are based on the following passage.

"You have a new baby," announced Ben.

Catching her, he trembled. He held her, a jewel, in his palms. "It's a girl," he said. "She's beautiful."

"A girl," said Jimmy Perez.

"Thank God you were here," exclaimed the glass-eyed woman, her pupil crackling with light.

"Let me," said Doris. "Let me see her."

Ben ran a finger inside the baby's mouth, then blew in her face to startle her. Next he turned her upside down, his hand locked around her ankles, flicked the bottoms of her feet gently, then slapped her on the back. The girl began to wriggle in his grasp and made small squawking noises. She turned pink gradually. When she started to cry, her father crossed himself. "A miracle," he said.

From *East of the Mountains*, by David Guterson

Write your answers to the questions below.

1. How did the baby's father react when the baby started to cry?

   _____

   _____

2. The glass-eyed woman says, "Thank God you were here." What does this suggest?

   _____

   _____

"Well, you wan't[1] using the roof," T.J. said. He paused a moment and added shrewdly, "so we thought to pretty it up a little bit."

"And sag it so I'd have to rebuild it," the man said sharply. He turned away, saying to a man beside him, "See that all that junk is shoveled off by tomorrow."

"Yes, sir," the man said.

T.J. started forward. "You can't do that," he said. "We toted[2] it up here, and it's our earth. We planted it and raised it and toted it up here."

The man stared at him coldly. "But it's my building," he said. "It's to be shoveled off tomorrow."

"It's our earth," T.J. said desperately. "You ain't got no right!"

[1] weren't
[2] brought

From "Antaeus," by Borden Deal

Circle the number of the correct answer.

3. What is the conflict in the story?

(1) T.J. doesn't like the owner of the building.

(2) T.J. has put soil on the roof, and the owner wants the soil off.

(3) The owner doesn't like to work with soil.

(4) The owner wants soil put on his roof, but no one will do it.

4. How does T.J. react to the building owner?

(1) T.J. thanks him.

(2) T.J. agrees with him.

(3) T.J. says nothing.

(4) T.J. argues with him.

Check your answers on page 165.

theme
the central idea of a
piece of writing

The central idea of a piece of writing is its **theme**. The theme of a story or poem is often a message about life. Common themes are "friendship is priceless" and "dreams are important to have."

Sometimes the theme of a story is stated directly. At the end of *The Wizard of Oz*, Dorothy says, "There's no place like home." This statement is the central idea of the story.

Read the paragraph. Underline the sentences that tell about the theme.

> "But man is not made for defeat," he said. "A man can be destroyed but not defeated." I am sorry that I killed the fish though, he thought. Now the bad time is coming and I do not even have the harpoon. The *dentuso*[1] is cruel and able and strong and intelligent. But I was more intelligent than he was. Perhaps not, he thought. Perhaps I was only better armed.
>
> [1] a mackerel shark
>
> From *The Old Man and the Sea*, by Ernest Hemingway

Sometimes the theme is not stated directly. You need to look at story elements such as character, plot, and setting, and think about how they relate to each other. For example, a story may tell of a man walking in the desert. He thinks about friends he once had until he turned against them. Suddenly, a snake springs up and bites him. As he falls down in pain, he wishes his old friends were near to help him. The setting, the plot, and the character support the theme: We need friends in our lives.

You can sometimes find the theme by thinking only about the main character. Does he or she learn a lesson or change in some way? If so, this is the theme of the story.

Check your answers on page 165.

The **mood** of a story is the feeling you get from what you are reading. Suppose you are reading a story about a man going down some basement stairs. Spider webs brush against his face. A step creaks under his foot. A strange shadow moves across the wall, as a cold wind raises the hair on the back of the man's neck.

Did you feel a little fear as you read? The writer has created a scary mood with details such as spider webs, a creaking step, a shadow, and a cold wind.

A story's mood doesn't always stay the same. For example, the story about the man continues. As he reaches the bottom of the stairs, the lights come on. The basement is decorated with streamers. A group of people dressed in party hats jump out, yelling, "Surprise!" The story's mood has changed. It is now happy.

mood
the feeling a piece of writing creates

Read the paragraph. Then answer the questions.

> But one day a change came over the woods and the pond. Warm air, soft and kind, blew through the trees. The ice, which had softened during the night, began to melt. Patches of open water appeared. All the creatures that lived in the pond and in the woods were glad to feel the warmth. They heard and felt the breath of spring, and they stirred with new life and hope. There was a good, new smell in the air, a smell of earth waking after its long sleep.
>
> From *The Trumpet of the Swan*, by E. B. White

1. What feeling did you get as you read the paragraph?

   _____

2. List two details that create this mood.

   _____

   _____

▶ GED **Tip**

To find the theme of a passage on the GED Reading Test, think about the main message of the piece.

Check your answers on page 165.

Questions 1–3 are based on the following passage.

Now the tension which had been growing in Juana boiled up to the surface and her lips were thin. "This thing is evil," she cried harshly. "This pearl is like a sin! It will destroy us," and her voice rose shrilly. "Throw it away, Kino. Let us break it between stones. Let us bury it and forget the place. Let us throw it back into the sea. It has brought evil. Kino, my husband, it will destroy us." And in the firelight her lips and her eyes were alive with her fear.

But Kino's face was set, and his mind and his will were set. "This is our one chance," he said. "Our son must go to school. He must break out of the pot that holds us in."

"It will destroy us all," Juana cried. "Even our son."

From *The Pearl*, by John Steinbeck

Write your answers to the questions below.

1. Why does Juana want to get rid of the pearl?

   _____

   _____

2. Why does Kino want to keep the pearl?

   _____

   _____

3. What is the theme of the passage?

   _____

   _____

Questions 4–5 are based on the following passage.

The huts looked like ghosts in the cold light. As we neared them I heard a strange sound like that of running feet. I thought that it was a sound made by the wind, but when we came closer I saw dozens of wild dogs scurrying around through the huts. They ran from us, snarling as they went.

The pack must have slunk into the village soon after we left, for it had gorged itself upon the abalone[1] we had not taken. It had gone everywhere searching out food, and Ramo and I had to look hard to find enough for our supper. While we ate beside a small fire I could hear the dogs on the hill not far away, and through the night their howls came to me on the wind.

[1] a type of shellfish that can be eaten

From *Island of the Blue Dolphins*, by Scott O'Dell

Circle the number of the correct answer.

4. What mood is created in this passage?

   (1) a spiritual mood
   (2) an uneasy mood
   (3) an adventurous mood
   (4) an angry mood

5. Which detail supports the mood of the passage?

   (1) We ate beside a small fire.
   (2) It had gone everywhere searching out food.
   (3) I had to look hard to find enough for supper.
   (4) The huts looked like ghosts in the cold light.

Check your answers on page 166.

Think about a song you love. What do you love about the song? Do the words have a special meaning to you? Do you like the way the words sound or the beat of the music? What do you picture when you hear the song?

In many ways, poems are like songs. Sound and **imagery** are important in both songs and poetry.

The sound of a poem comes from the words the poet chooses. Many poems have words that **rhyme**. Words that rhyme sound alike, such as *tall* and *fall*, or *new* and *grew*. Most poems also have a **rhythm**, or repeating beat.

Just like fiction is divided into paragraphs, poems are often divided into **stanzas**. Each stanza is a grouping of lines in the poem.

Read the poem. Circle the words that rhyme. Then answer the question.

imagery
pictures that come to mind while reading

rhyme
words that sound alike, such as *go, no,* and *show*

rhythm
the beat of a poem

stanza
a grouping of lines in a poem

Some People

Isn't it strange some people make
   You feel so tired inside,
Your thoughts begin to shrivel up
   Like leaves all brown and dried!

But when you're with some other ones,
   It's stranger still to find
Your thoughts as thick as fireflies
   All shiny in your mind!

by Rachel Field, *POEMS*

How many stanzas are in the poem?

_____

Check your answers on page 166.

Imagery is created through the use of strong, colorful words. Some imagery comes from words that appeal to one or more of the senses of sight, touch, smell, sound, and taste. A **phrase** such as "screeching wheels" helps you to imagine the sound wheels make. The phrase "fluttering chicks" helps you to picture small birds and how they move.

phrase
a group of two or more words, but not a complete sentence

Read each phrase and think about what comes to mind. Then circle all of the senses that each phrase appeals to.

1. a bright red rose

    sight   touch   smell   sound   taste

2. thick, sweet cream

    sight   touch   smell   sound   taste

3. a bird's cheerful song

    sight   touch   smell   sound   taste

Imagery can also be created in other ways. One way is to compare things that are different. A poem may say, "The clouds are spun cotton candy." Here, clouds are compared to cotton candy. You probably picture the clouds as looking swirled and fluffy like cotton candy.

Write the two things that are being compared in each sentence.

4. The sun is a lamp in the east.

    _____

5. The bee sting burned like fire.

    _____

Check your answers on page 166.

GED Tip

When reading a poem on the GED Reading Test, look for comparisons and focus on the images created by the words.

Practice

Questions 1–3 are based on the following stanza of poetry.

> Oh, I have seen the dawn above a mountain
> > That floods a plain,
> Where life wells up, like water from a fountain,
> > All sweet again,
> Have seen the world awaken like a child
> > With eyes of blue,
> That stretched its arms, breathed deeply then, and smiled
> > That night was through.
>
> From "Waking of a City", by Douglas Malloch,
> *The Art and Craft of Poetry*

Circle the number of the correct answer.

1. In the poem, what is life compared to?

   (1) a child

   (2) the night

   (3) water

   (4) a plain

2. Which of the following lines compares two things?

   (1) That stretched its arms, breathed deeply then, and smiled

   (2) Have seen the world awaken like a child

   (3) Oh, I have seen the dawn above a mountain

   (4) both (1) and (2)

3. What is the poem saying about the dawn?

   (1) It is a sad time of day.

   (2) It is a noisy time of day.

   (3) It is a hopeful time of day.

   (4) It is a child's favorite time of day.

Questions 4–6 are based on the following poem.

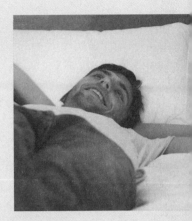

Dreams

Hold fast to dreams
For if dreams die
Life is a broken-winged bird
That cannot fly.

Hold fast to dreams
For when dreams go
Life is a barren field
Frozen with snow.

by Langston Hughes, *The Dream Keeper and other Poems*

Circle the number of the correct answer.

4. In the first stanza, what is a life without dreams compared to?

   (1) sleep
   (2) a broken-winged bird
   (3) a fly
   (4) a dead bird

5. In the last stanza, what is a life without dreams compared to?

   (1) snow
   (2) a dream
   (3) a barren field
   (4) a pond

6. The words "a barren field / Frozen with snow" appeal to
   which senses?

   (1) sight and taste
   (2) sound and smell
   (3) touch and sound
   (4) sight and touch

Check your answers on page 166.

GED Skill Strategy

Understanding Fiction Passages

When you understand a fiction passage, you know who the characters are. You have an idea about how they look and why they act the way they do.

 Strategy Read the passage. Ask yourself: Who is the main character? What do I know about this character?

1. Find out what you can about how the main character looks.

2. Notice how the main character acts.

3. Think about the main character's personality, or traits.

Exercise 1:   Read the paragraph. Answer the questions.

Through the years, Kate had seen Seth only at his office in the city. There, they had talked about Kate's health and medical care. Now they talked about sore joints and their grandchildren. During her last visit, Seth had invited Kate to his house for a small dinner party. She paced her kitchen as she thought about visiting Seth at his house. They had only known each other as doctor and patient. But, by gosh, Kate intended to go!

1. Who is the main character?

   _____

2. Which detail gives a clue to the main character's age?

   _____

3. How do you know that the main character is nervous?

   _____

   _____

Knowing when and where an event takes place in a story helps you understand what you read. It also helps you picture the setting.

 Strategy Read the passage. Ask yourself: Where and when is this event taking place? What happens in the story?

1. Look for clues that tell you where the event takes place.

2. Look for clues that tell you when the event takes place.

3. Think about the important things that happen in the story.

Exercise 2:   Read the passage. Answer the questions.

> Kate walked through Seth's house out to the backyard. The house was on a lake, and the setting sun shone on the water. Kate didn't see Seth at first, and then he was taking her hand and thanking her for coming.
>
> People surrounded her as Seth made the introductions. "Kate, meet my daughter, Liz, and my grandson, Alex."

1. Where are the characters?

   _____

2. How do you know what time of day it is?

   _____

3. What happens in this passage?

   _____

   _____

   _____

Check your answers on page 167.

GED Test-Taking Strategy

Using Line Numbers

On the GED Reading Test, the lines of passages and poems have line numbers next to them. Some questions refer to specific lines.

 Strategy   Try this strategy with the following example. Use these steps.

Step 1   Read the question. Notice the line numbers in it.

Step 2   To find the right line, count from the nearest line number.

Step 3   Read the information and answer the question.

Example

WHAT DID THE BULL ALLIGATOR DO?

Suddenly the water roiled, and a monstrous bull alligator thrashed to the surface with a snapping turtle in his mouth. He swung his whole body from side to side like a huge killing machine. The turtle broke into pieces. The bull
(5)   swallowed. The canoe rocked so hard, I grabbed the gunwale[1] to steady it. Other 'gators' eyes popped up around me like submarine periscopes[2]. They moved forward. I backwatered, turned, and paddled home.

From *Tree Castle Island*, by Jean Craighead George

[1] upper edge of a boat   [2] tools for looking above water when you are underwater

In lines 3–4, what is the swinging bull alligator compared to?

(1) a snapping turtle
(2) a submarine periscope
(3) a monstrous bull
(4) a huge killing machine

In Step 1 you read the question and noticed the line numbers. In Step 2 you counted the lines. In Step 3 you answered the question based on the information in those lines. Choices (1), (2), and (3) are all found in the passage, but only Choice (4) is in lines 3–4.

Practice

Practice the strategy. Use the steps you have learned. Circle the number of the correct answer.

HOW DOES THE NARRATOR FEEL ON A SKATEBOARD?

          Skimming
        an asphalt sea
     I swerve, I curve, I
    sway; I speed to whirring
(5)   sound an inch above the
      ground; I'm the sailor
      and the sail, I'm the
     driver and the wheel
     I'm the one and only
(10)   single engine
      human auto
       mobile.

"The Sidewalk Racer, or On the Skateboard,"
by Lillian Morrison

1. What is the asphalt sea in line 2?

  (1) a fish
  (2) an automobile
  (3) a skateboard
  (4) the road

2. What is the skateboarder compared to in line 6?

  (1) a sailor
  (2) a driver
  (3) an engine
  (4) an automobile

Check your answers on page 167.

Read each selection and question carefully. Circle the number of the correct answer.

<u>Questions 1–2 are based on the following passage.</u>

WHAT DOES THE SOLDIER WANT?

Even though my knees were trembly with fear, I stood and faced the soldier. "What do you want? Why don't you say something?"

He raised his head slowly and looked at me. His eyes were glassy, unfocused, his face deathly white under a layer of grime. Despite his beard and long hair, I could see he wasn't much older than Avery—eighteen, nineteen. Surely not over twenty.

My fear eased a bit, and I loosened my death grip on the milk bucket. "What do you want?" I asked again.

"Food," he croaked in a low voice. "And shelter ... Please."

From *Hear the Wind Blow*, by Mary Downing Hahn

1. What does the soldier want from the narrator?

   (1) a horse and a gun
   (2) a bath and a shave
   (3) food and shelter
   (4) news about the war

2. Which two words describe the soldier?

   (1) clean and handsome
   (2) old and threatening
   (3) young and angry
   (4) young and bearded

Questions 3–5 are based on the following paragraph.

DO THESE MEN LIKE EACH OTHER?

All was still. The only sound was the clear, lonely song of a spring bird in the darkness outside. Though a faint breeze blew in from the window the air in the room was sour and close. There was a feeling both of tenseness and exhaustion. Doctor Copeland leaned forward from the pillow. His eyes were bloodshot and his hands clutched the counterpane[1]. The neck of his nightshirt had slipped down over his bony shoulder. Jake's heels were balanced on the rungs of his chair and his giant hands folded between his knees in a waiting and childlike attitude. Deep black circles were beneath his eyes, his hair was unkempt. They looked at each other and waited. As the silence grew longer the tenseness between them became more strained.

[1] bedspread

From *The Heart is a Lonely Hunter*, by Carson McCullers

3. Which detail gives a clue about when the events take place?

(1) All was still.
(2) Doctor Copeland leaned forward from the pillow.
(3) They looked at each other and waited.
(4) The only sound was the clear, lonely song of a spring bird.

4. During what time of day do the events take place?

(1) in the morning
(2) noon
(3) in the afternoon
(4) just before dawn

5. Which word best describes the mood of the paragraph?

(1) calm
(2) angry
(3) fearful
(4) tense

Question 6 is based on the following poem.

WHAT IS A PEACH LIKE?

Peach

Touch it to your cheek and it's soft
as a velvet newborn mouse
who has to strive
to be alive.

Bite in. Runny
honey
blooms on your tongue—
as if you've bitten open
a whole hive.

From *Knock at a Star*, by Rose Rauter

6. To what senses does the poem appeal?

(1) hearing and taste

(2) touch and taste

(3) sight and smell

(4) smell and taste

Check your answers on page 167.

Unit 5 Skill Check-Up Chart

Check your answers. In the first column, circle the numbers of any questions that you have missed. Then look across the rows to see the skills you need to review and the pages where you can find each skill.

Question	Skill	Page
2, 3, 4	Understanding Character and Setting	114–117
1	Understanding Plot and Conflict	118–121
5	Understanding Theme and Mood	122–125
6	Understanding Imagery in Poetry	126–129

Posttest

This *Reading Posttest* will give you an idea of how well you've learned to apply the reading skills in this book. You will read short passages and answer multiple-choice questions. There is no time limit.

Read each passage and question carefully. Circle the number of the correct answer.

Questions 1–2 are based on the following paragraph.

> **HOW DO YOU WORK THIS STOVE?**
>
> Some stoves have a timer that will turn the oven on automatically. If you want to use the timer on an oven, first make sure that the main clock is set for the correct time. Second, turn the control knob to "Timed Bake."
> (5) Third, set the start dial for the time that the oven should turn on. Fourth, set the stop dial for the time that the oven should turn off. Finally, check that the oven is set for the correct temperature.

1. After reading the first two sentences, what could you predict the paragraph would be about?

    (1) setting a timer
    (2) setting a clock
    (3) turning off the oven
    (4) checking the oven's temperature

2. What should you do before setting the stop dial for the time that the oven should turn off?

    (1) Check that the oven is set for the correct temperature.
    (2) Set the start dial for the time that the oven should turn on.
    (3) Turn the control knob to "Off."
    (4) Set the main clock for the time that the oven should turn on.

Questions 3–4 are based on the following poem.

WHAT WERE THESE WOMEN LIKE?

Women

They were women then
My mama's generation
Husky of voice—Stout of
Step
With fists as well as
Hands
How they battered down
Doors
And ironed
Starched white
Shirts
How they led
Armies
Headragged Generals
Across mined
Fields
Boobytrapped
Ditches
To discover books
Desks
A place for us
How they knew what we
Must know
Without knowing a page
Of it
Themselves.

by Alice Walker

3. What does the theme of the poem say about past women?

   (1) They had to break into the military.
   (2) They had to iron and do lots of other things.
   (3) They had to learn to read.
   (4) They had to fight to improve things for everyone.

4. "Husky of voice—Stout of/Step" appeals to the sense of

   (1) smell.
   (2) touch.
   (3) sound.
   (4) taste.

Questions 5–6 are based on the following paragraph.

WHAT KIND OF ADVICE DOES THIS PARAGRAPH PROVIDE?

(5)   When someone is arrested, he or she has the right to ask for a lawyer. The person also has the right not to answer certain questions that might incriminate that person, or make that person appear guilty. The police must tell the person his or her rights. If the police do not, nothing the person says can be used as evidence in court.

5. The word *incriminate* on line 3 means to

   (1) make someone appear guilty.
   (2) decide not to answer questions.
   (3) arrest someone.
   (4) use as evidence in court.

6. Which of the following can you infer?

   (1) People who are arrested do not have any rights.
   (2) After a person is read his or her rights, anything he or she says can be used as evidence in court.
   (3) Most people who are arrested remain silent.
   (4) Most people who are arrested incriminate themselves.

Questions 7–9 are based on the following article.

WHAT DO THESE HINTS HELP YOU TO DO?

Helen's Hints: A Little Something Unusual Might Help!

People write all the time telling me that they have trouble starting a conversation with someone they don't know. One solution is to get other people to talk to you. You can wear or carry something unusual or

(5) interesting. Someone may have something to say about a T-shirt with a funny saying on it. An unusual pin, tie, ring, or hat may give someone a reason to ask you a question. It's much easier to say, "I've never seen a ring like that. What is it made of?" than to say,

(10) "Hi, I'm Marta."

7. What is the main idea of the article?

(1) There are some easy ways to get people to start talking to you.

(2) People write to Helen all the time.

(3) Some problems are easy to solve.

(4) Some people have trouble talking to people they don't know.

8. According to Helen, what is an unusual or interesting thing that you can wear or carry?

(1) a T-shirt with a funny saying

(2) a trick tie clip

(3) an expensive wedding ring

(4) a list of conversation starters

9. One way to get people to talk to you is to

(1) ask them questions.

(2) introduce yourself by name.

(3) tease others about the style of their clothing.

(4) wear something unusual.

Questions 10–12 are based on the following letter.

WHAT DOES THIS LETTER WRITER BELIEVE?

Dear Editor:

About 25 percent of the people in the United States smoke. Most smokers are considerate. They understand that some people do not like smoke, and they try not to smoke near them. However, there are
(5) many laws that restrict smoking. In some cases, smokers may only smoke outside. They may not smoke in restaurants and other public places. You always hear nonsmokers scream about their "right" to breathe clean air. I believe that smokers have rights,
(10) too! Their right to smoke should be respected.

Sincerely,

Angela Bertelli

10. A person who is *considerate* (line 2) is someone who

   (1) cares about other people's feelings.
   (2) bothers other people.
   (3) likes to smoke.
   (4) believes that smokers have rights too.

11. Which sentence from the letter shows the writer's bias?

   (1) There are many laws that restrict smoking.
   (2) They may not smoke in restaurants.
   (3) About 25 percent of the people in the U.S. smoke.
   (4) Nonsmokers scream about their "right" to breathe clean air.

12. Which of these expresses an opinion of the letter writer?

   (1) However, there are many laws that restrict smoking.
   (2) Smokers may not smoke in restaurants.
   (3) I believe that smokers have rights, too!
   (4) In some cases, smokers may only smoke outside.

Questions 13–15 are based on the following work rules.

WHAT TYPE OF EMPLOYEE INFORMATION IS IN THESE RULES?

Employee Working Hours

All county employees work a 5-day, 40-hour week.
On-call employees must respond to all emergencies. Failure to act may result in job loss or disciplinary action.

Overtime Pay Options

If an employee works more than 40 hours per week, pay options are as follows:

- Hourly employees receive either additional vacation time or overtime pay (time and a half per hour worked).
- Managers work additional hours as needed without additional vacation time or overtime pay.

13. What is the main point of the work rules?

    (1) emergency calls and how they should be handled

    (2) working hours and overtime pay options

    (3) the duties of managers

    (4) the hours employees are expected to work each week

14. An hourly employee working more than forty hours could be given

    (1) a pay raise.

    (2) overtime pay.

    (3) a managerial job.

    (4) disciplinary action.

15. What may result if an emergency call is not answered?

    (1) job loss

    (2) overtime pay

    (3) additional vacation time

    (4) assignment of additional work hours

Questions 16–17 are based on the following passage.

HOW DO BANKS TREAT SAVINGS ACCOUNTS AND LOANS DIFFERENTLY?

Many people deposit money in a savings account that earns interest. Interest is paid by the bank to the holder of the savings account. The amount of interest earned depends on how much money is in the account.
(5)   Banks pay interest to account holders because the bank uses their money to make loans. People might need a loan to buy a car, pay bills, or even start a new business.
When people take out a loan from a bank, they must pay it back. They must also pay interest to the bank. The
(10)   amount of interest charged depends on how much money is borrowed. A bank charges more interest to borrowers than it pays to savings account holders.

16. The word *deposit* in line 1 of the passage means to

(1) put money into a bank.
(2) bring something to a certain place.
(3) leave something somewhere for safekeeping.
(4) give a sum of money as part of a payment.

17. How does the amount of interest charged on a loan compare to the interest earned on a savings account?

(1) The amount of interest charged for a loan is higher.
(2) The amount of interest charged for a loan is lower.
(3) The amount of interest charged for a loan is about the same.
(4) The amount of interest charged for a loan is three times higher.

Questions 18–20 are based on the following paragraph.

WHAT HAS HAPPENED TO THIS YOUNG MAN?

It was bright sunlight in the room when I woke. I thought I was back at the front[1] and stretched out in bed. My legs hurt me and I looked down at them still in the dirty bandages, and seeing them knew where I was. I reached up for the bell-cord and pushed the button. I heard it buzz down the hall and then someone coming on rubber soles along the hall. It was Miss Gage and she looked a little older in the bright sunshine and not so pretty.

From *A Farewell to Arms*, by Ernest Hemingway

[1] an area where two armies are fighting.

18. From the paragraph, you can conclude that the narrator

    (1) has bandages on his hands.

    (2) can not reach the bell-cord.

    (3) does not know where he is.

    (4) is in a hospital.

19. What is the narrator's main problem?

    (1) He was injured in a battle.

    (2) He wants to return to the front.

    (3) He has lost the use of his legs.

    (4) He needs more help than Miss Gage can provide.

20. When do the events in the paragraph take place?

    (1) at night

    (2) during the day

    (3) before dawn

    (4) after sunset

When you have finished the *Reading Posttest*, check your answers on page 168. Then look at the chart on page 145.

Skills Review Chart

This chart shows you which skills you should review. Check your answers. In the first column, circle the number of any questions you missed. Then look across the row to find out which skills you should review as well as the page numbers on which you find instruction on those skills. Compare the items you circled in the *Skills Review Chart* to those you circled in the *Skills Preview Chart* to see the progress you've made.

Questions	Skill	Pages
8	Scanning	12–17
1	Predicting	18–23
5, 10	Using Context Clues	24–31
16	Understanding Multiple Meanings	32–35
7	Finding the Stated Main Idea	44–49
13	Determining the Implied Main Idea	50–53
14	Locating Supporting Details	54–57
2	Showing Time Order	66–69
17	Comparing and Contrasting	70–73
15	Showing Cause and Effect	74–77
9	Giving Examples	78–81
6	Making Inferences	90–93
18	Drawing Conclusions	94–97
12	Identifying Fact and Opinion	98–101
11	Detecting Bias	102–105
20	Understanding Character and Setting	114–117
19	Understanding Plot and Conflict	118–121
3	Understanding Theme and Mood	122–125
4	Understanding Imagery in Poetry	126–129

Glossary

article a complete piece of writing in a magazine or newspaper. *page 19*

bias strong feeling for or against something. *page 102*

capitalize to begin a word with a capital letter. *page 13*

cause why something happens. *page 74*

chapter the parts that a book is divided into. *page 20*

characters the people in a story. *page 114*

chronological order arranged in order by time—what happened first, second, third, and so on. *page 66*

compare showing how things are alike. *page 70*

conflict a struggle between two opposing forces. *page 119*

context the words and sentences that help you figure out the meaning of an unfamiliar word. *page 24*

contrast showing how things are different. *page 70*

definition an explanation of a word's meaning. *page 25*

draw a conclusion figure out something based on facts, inferences, and what you already know about a subject. *page 94*

educated guess a guess you make based on what you already know. *page 21*

effect a result or outcome; what happens. *page 74*

event something that happens, especially something exciting, unusual, or interesting. *page 118*

evidence information that proves something is true. *page 91*

fact something that is true or can be proved. *page 98*

illustrate make clear, explain, or give examples. *page 78*

imagery pictures that come to mind while reading. *page 126*

implied unwritten or unspoken. *page 50*

imply does not directly state; suggest. *page 90*

indented writing that is set in from the normal starting place. *page 44*

infer figure out from given information. *page 90*

influence affect the way a person thinks. *page 102*

introduction a book or a paragraph's beginning that prepares people for what they will read. *page 46*

limited not everything about the subject is included or explained. *page 45*

loaded word a word that creates an emotional response. *page 102*

main character the central character in a story. *page 114*

mood the feeling a piece of writing creates. *page 123*

neutral showing no feeling for or against something. *page 103*

opinion what a person thinks, believes, or feels about something. *page 98*

organized arranged in a certain way. *page 66*

paragraph a group of one or more sentences about one idea or topic. *pages 12 and 44*

passage a short piece of writing that is several paragraphs long. *page 12*

phrase a group of two or more words, but not a complete sentence. *pages 67 and 127*

plot a series of actions or events; what happens in a story. *page 118*

predict to use information you know to guess what will happen later. *page 18*

proper name a name used for a particular person, place, or thing. A proper name always begins with a capital letter. *page 14*

prove show that something is true. *page 54*

punctuation marks that make sentences easier to understand. Periods, commas, dashes, and colons are examples of punctuation. *page 26*

rhyme words that sound alike, such as *go, no,* and *show*. *page 126*

rhythm the beat of a poem. *page 126*

scanning quickly running your eyes over a passage to look for specific information. *page 12*

sequence the order in which things are done or happen. *page 66*

setting where and when events in a story take place. *page 115*

specific particular; a certain kind. *page 12*

stanza a grouping of lines in a poem. *page 126*

stated written or spoken. *page 50*

supporting details details that explain, prove, or give information about the main idea. *page 54*

table of contents a listing of the articles found in a magazine or a listing of the parts of a book. *page 19*

theme the central idea of a piece of writing. *page 122*

topic the subject, or main idea. *page 45*

topic sentence the sentence that gives the main idea of the paragraph. *page 46*

traits a person's qualities. *page 114*

Answers and Explanations

Page 3

1. **(1) June 1, 1937** Choices (2) and (3) are incorrect because these dates tell when Earhart arrived in New Guinea and when she left New Guinea, not when she began her trip. Choice (4) is incorrect because this date does not appear in the paragraph.

2. **(3) Her last flight was meant to take her around the world.** The word *meant* implies that Earhart had intended to do something but did not do it. Choices (1) and (2) are true statements from the paragraph, but they do not suggest that Earhart will not complete her trip. Choice (4) is not a suggestion, but a fact, and it is not the first hint in the paragraph that Earhart's flight was not completed.

3. **(2) Puerto Rico** Choice (1) is incorrect because this was where Earhart's flight began. Choice (3) is incorrect because Africa was where Earhart stopped after South America. Choice (4) is not correct because this was Earhart's last stop.

Page 4

4. **(4) clouds of ash blocking the sun.** Nuclear winter is caused by the blocking of the sun's rays with dust and smoke in the atmosphere. Choices (1), (2), and (3) are all results, not causes, of nuclear winter.

5. **(2) dust and soot.** In the fourth sentence, the word *ash* has the same meaning as *dust* and *soot*. The words "These clouds of ash" refer to the dust and soot mentioned in the third sentence. Choices (1), (3), and (4) are all incorrect because these meanings do not fit the context in the sentence.

6. **(3) temperatures to lower.** Because the warmth of the sun's rays would be blocked and plants and animals would freeze, you can conclude that the planet's temperature would grow lower, or colder. Choices (1), (2), and (4) are not supported by the information in the paragraph.

7. **(4) a food product grown on a farm** While Choices (1), (2), and (3) are all definitions of the word *crop*, only Choice (4) gives the meaning of the word as it is used in the paragraph.

Page 5

8. **(3) The mayor has failed to keep her promise.** Choices (1), (2), and (4) are all details that support the main idea.

9. **(1) took bribes.** This is one of the examples given in the letter. Choice (2) is not mentioned in the paragraph. Choices (3) and (4) are things that the mayor, not the officials, has done.

10. **(2) The mayor has let us all down.** This statement tells what the letter writer thinks or feels, expressing an opinion. Choices (1), (3), and (4) are all facts that can be proven.

11. **(3) Think about this when you vote next month!** This detail tells you voters will have a chance to vote for Smith soon. You can infer that she is running again for mayor next month. Choices (1) and (2) are incorrect because they do not give information that suggests Smith is running for mayor again. Therefore, Choice (4) is also not correct.

12. **(1) a change in a man's health insurance rate.** The letter mainly tells about an increase in Mr. Stuart's health insurance payment. Choices (2), (3), and (4) are details that support the main idea.

13. **(3) turns a certain age** Choices (1) and (2) tell what insurance rates are based on. However, the only time these factors are reviewed is when a policy holder turns a certain age. Choice (4) is incorrect because Choices (1) and (2) are incorrect.

14. **(2) five years ago.** The letter tells that Mr. Stuart just turned 50. It also tells you that insurance rates are reviewed at certain ages that are five years apart. You can use this information to figure out that Mr. Collins' last review was when he was 45—five years ago.

15. **(1) enthusiastic** The writer says that Foxx's performance is "brilliant," "incredible," and that his performance is one you won't soon forget. This tells you that the writer was enthusiastic about his performance. Choice (2) is too mild; it does not fully reflect the writer's praise. Choices (3) and (4) are incorrect because they tell the opposite of what the writer feels.

16. **(2) It shows both sides of Charles's character.** When comparing *Ray* with movies about other musicians, the writer that "*Ray* . . . presents a story about a man who is a brilliant musician but a flawed human being." Choices (1), (3), and (4) are incorrect because they are not supported by the details in the review.

17. **(2) He is brilliant.** The writer compares Foxx's performance in *Ray* with his performance in other movies by saying that Foxx "serves up yet another inspired performance." Choices (1), (3), and (4) are not mentioned in the review.

18. **(3) on the subway** The first sentence of the second paragraph states that the boys are on the platform. You can figure out from this and other clues about a platform that the story takes place on a subway. Choices (1), (2), and (4) are mentioned, but they do not refer to the setting of the passage.

19. **(2) the man on the train who once hopped on moving trucks.** Most of the passage tells how the boys on the subway are similar to a man who is a passenger. We learn that this man was once a tough boy and that he finished high school, married, and was in a good job and going to school. Since this character is the focus of the passage, it is likely that most of the plot will focus on him. Choice (1) is incorrect because the first paragraph already gives the reader information about tough boys. Choices (3) and (4) are incorrect because these ideas are only details in the passage that the writer does not explore further.

20. **(4) lonely** Many of the words in the poem—*desolate, lone, lost, tears, trouble*—suggest loneliness. Choice (1) is incorrect because the mood does not suggest bitterness, but the feeling of being lost and alone. Choice (2) is incorrect because the images do not create a feeling of hopefulness. Choice (3) is incorrect because the images in the poem do not create an angry mood.

21. (1) a helpless and abandoned feeling.
A way to show the helpless feeling of loneliness is to compare the sound of a lone boat in the fog to a lost child calling out for help. Choices (2) and (4) are images that come to mind in the poem, but not from the comparison of a boat's whistle and a lost child. Choice (3) is not an idea suggested in the poem.

Unit 1 Lesson 1

Page 12

Ads for $950 and less: BIG 1 Bedrm.; BRIGHT, 2 bedrm.; WOMAN seeks rmmate.

Page 14

1. $15.00

2. January 15

Page 15

(3) It protects them and their patients from germs. Choices (1) and (2) are incorrect because they are not mentioned in the paragraph. Choice (4) is another use of a uniform besides protection.

Page 16

1. Lavalle Household Products
293 Bloomfield Ave.
Montclair, NJ 07043

2. **(4) the name of a business and an address.** Choices (1), (2), and (3) are incorrect because they would not give you enough information to write and mail a letter of complaint.

3. **(2) First Aid.** Choices (1) and 3 are incorrect because they are warnings. Choice (4) is incorrect because it is an instruction.

4. **(3) To clean** Choices (1), (2), and (4) are incorrect because they are not directions on how to use the product to clean.

Page 17

5. **(4) Helen Keller** Choices (1), (2), and (3) are incorrect because only Helen Keller had two disabilities.

6. **(2) Sarah Bernhardt lost her leg.** Choice (1) is not correct because this happened in 1933. Choices (3) and (4) are incorrect because no dates are given in the passage for when these things happened.

7. **(3) He had polio.** Choice (1) refers to Toulouse-Lautrec. Choice (2) is incorrect because it is not mentioned in the paragraph. Choice (4) is incorrect because Choices (1) and (2) are incorrect.

Lesson 2

Page 20

1. ways you could use a computer

2. Chapter 3, The Mechanics of Computers

Page 22

1. **(2) *The Official Guidebook of Soccer Rules*** Choice (1) gives the history of track and field, not useful rules for coaching. Choices (3) and (4) give information on sports figures, not coaching.

2. **(1) *Home Accidents—What to Do in an Emergency*** Choice (2) is incorrect because this book gives you tips about staying safe, not emergency procedures. Choice (3) does not give you information on household problems. Choice (4) is incorrect because Choice (2) is not a correct choice.

3. **(3) Landlords Against New Rent-Control Laws** Choices (1), (2), and (4) do not involve new laws.

4. **(4) Article 4** Choices (1), (2), and (3) are incorrect because these articles will not help you find an apartment.

Page 23

Information Needed	Book	Chapter
what to do if you want to sell your car	2	You and Your Property
what to do if the sink drain is clogged	1	Pipes, Drains, and Leaky Faucets
what to do if all the lights go out	1	Wires and Switches
what to do if you are renting an apartment and get an eviction notice	2	You and Your Landlord

Lesson 3

Page 25

a place where birds are kept

Page 26

1. able to change behavior to suit a situation

2. the dash (—) after the word *adaptable*

To avoid repeating a word, you might use a synonym, a word that has the same or almost the same meaning as another word.

3. synonym

4. a word that has the same or almost the same meaning as another word

5. a comma

Page 27

1. clothing

2. The words after the dash give examples of clothing.

Page 28

1. noisy

2. quietly

3. There are many possible answers. Here is an example: George is usually unkempt. His shirt is never tucked in, and his shoes are often untied.

Page 29

1. **(3) a group of people who get together to fight something they think is unfair.** Choices (1), (2), and (4) are incorrect because they do not agree with the definition of *protest* given in the fifth sentence of the paragraph.

2. **(2) sent away.** Choices (1), (3), and (4) are incorrect because they do not agree with the definition of *suspended* suggested in the last sentence of the paragraph.

Page 30

3. **(2) "and had to return home."** Choices (1) and (4) are incorrect because they do not apply to the word. Choice (3) is in the same sentence but has an opposite meaning because it comes after *instead*.

4. **(1) in power.** Choices (2), (3), and (4) are incorrect because they do not agree with the meaning of *authorities* suggested in the third sentence of the paragraph.

5. **(3) school.** Choices (1), (2), and (4) are incorrect because they do not agree with the meaning suggested for *college* in the second sentence of the paragraph.

6. **(4) "students" and "their school."** Choices (1), (2), and (3) are incorrect because they do not tell about the word *college*.

7. **(3) talk into.** Choices (1), (2), and (4) are incorrect because they do not agree with the meaning suggested for *convince* in the sixth sentence of the paragraph.

8. **(2) a person in the same group.** Choices (1), (3), and (4) are incorrect because they do not make sense in the context of the phrase, "Nelson helped convince his fellow students."

Page 31

9. **(2) mud and sand that the river carries to different places along the river.** Choices (1), (3), and (4) are incorrect because they do not agree with the definition of *deposit* in the second and third sentences of the paragraph.

10. **(4) good for growing things.** Choices (1), (2), and (3) are incorrect because they do not agree with the meaning of fertile suggested by *rich* in the second sentence of the paragraph.

11. **(1) deposits that settle at the bottom of a body of water.** Choices (2), (3), and (4) are incorrect because they do not make sense in the context of the paragraph.

12. **(2) a land deposit at the mouth of a river.** Choice (1) is also a correct meaning of *delta*, but it is not the right meaning in the context of the sentence. Choices (3) and (4) are incorrect because they do not agree with the definition of *delta* given in the sixth sentence of the paragraph.

Lesson 4

Page 32

1. a word, phrase, or idea that explains why or how something happens

2. a young person, a child

Page 33

1. a metal instrument used to unlock a door

2. a young goat

3. to joke with or have fun with

Page 34

1. **(4) to fall down and lose consciousness** Choices (1), (2), and (3) are incorrect because they are descriptive words, not action words.

2. **(1) a kind of dance** Choices (2), (3), and (4) are incorrect because they are not related to dancing.

3. **(2) what remained** Choices (1), (3), and (4) are incorrect because they do not fit the context.

Page 35

4. **(2) a unit of measurement** Choices (1), (3), and (4) are incorrect because they do not involve measurement.

5. **(3) a machine used to weigh things** Choices (1), (2), and (4) are incorrect because they do not fit the context.

6. **(3) to strike out or remove** Choices (1), (2), and (4) are incorrect because they cannot apply to a list.

7. **(3) fruits and vegetables** Choices (1), (2), and (4) are incorrect because they cannot apply to a section of a grocery store containing cherries.

GED Skill Strategy, *pages 36–37*

Page 36

1. **(b)** someone who gives money to worthy causes or projects.

2. **(a)** book lover

Page 37

3. **a work stoppage by employees** This definition fits best because the paragraph is about something that workers could do.

4. **a big success** This definition fits best because it means that everyone loved the play, as the first sentence states.

GED Test-Taking Strategy

Page 39

1. **(3) A great deal of information is available on the Internet.** Choices (1), (2), and (4) provide correct information, but they do not answer the question. After previewing the question, you may have noticed "Information Superhighway" in the first sentence. The answer follows.

2. **(2) plans new shows** Choice (1) takes place in the morning and Choices (3) and (4) are things that Oprah talks about doing. She does not actually do them.

GED Test Practice, *pages 40–42*

Page 40

1. **(2) the order children are born in** Choices (1), (3), and (4) are not correct because they do not have anything to do with order. Order is suggested in the question above the paragraph.

2. **(2) the middle children** Choices (1), (3), and (4) are not correct because the passage tells you that middle children are the peacemakers.

3. **(3) "qualities"** Choices (1), (2), and (4) are not correct because they do not fit the meaning of *traits*. The definition of *traits* is provided in context. Commas help show where the definition is in the sentence.

Page 41

4. **(4)** *Disasters on the Great Lakes* Choices (1) and 2 are not about the Great Lakes. Choice (3) is not about shipwrecks or disasters. You are looking for information on a ship that sank, a disaster that happened on the Great Lakes.

5. **(4) "We are holding our own."** Choice (4) is the only correct answer. This answer can be found by scanning the passage for the words in each answer or by scanning for quotation marks.

6. **(3) a ship that carries goods from one place to another.** Choices (1), (2), and (4) do not make sense in the context of the passage. Choice (3) is the only correct answer. The carrier in this passage is a ship that hauled iron ore.

Page 42

7. **(2) grows the feathers needed to fly.** Choices (1), (3), and (4) do not make sense in the context of the passage. In the passage, dashes show you that the definition of *fledges* will follow.

8. **(3) to provide food for** Choices (1), (2), and (4) do not make sense in the context.

Unit 2 Lesson 5

Page 44

three

Page 45

(1)

Page 46

   There is a growing health care problem in the United States.

Page 47

1. Many people today think that knitting is just plain cool.

2. Example: a. The hobby has taken hold among people of all ages—teens, college students, and adults. b. Stars think it's cool, too.

Page 48

1. In 1956 the Supreme Court said blacks must have equal access to all interstate buses.

2. Any of the other sentences in the paragraph can be listed as one that tells more about the main idea.

Page 49

1. (2) The sentences in (1) are about injuries, but they don't have a theme that unifies them. The sentences in (2) all relate to one topic—the things you should do when a person is seriously injured.

2. Sentence 1: There are several things you can do to help a person who has been seriously injured.

3. Sentence 4: Glenn was about to travel in space around Earth.

Lesson 6

Page 50

(4) Eloy spends his time working and caring for his children. Choices (1), (2), and (3) are true but none tells what the paragraph is mostly about.

Page 51

1. (3) Phyllis takes good care of herself by exercising and watching what she eats. All the sentences tell about one main idea—that Phyllis takes good care of herself. Choices (1), (2), and (4) are incorrect because they are details that support the main idea.

2. (2) Technology helps people do their jobs. Choice (1) is not correct because the paragraph is not about cell phones only. Choice (3) is not an idea stated or hinted at in the paragraph. Choice (4) presents an opposite view that is the opposite of the ideas in the paragraph. The paragraph tells how technology helps business.

3. A sample answer would be:
The strange actions of animals helped predict an earthquake.

Page 52

1. (1) There is help for people who feel that they have been treated unfairly by a business. The first sentence explains that there is help for those who need it. The remaining sentences explain how to get help, supporting the first sentence.

2. (4) There is no topic sentence. All the sentences are about presidents and their dogs. No one sentence ties these sentences together.

Page 53

3. **(4) There is no topic sentence.** All the sentences seem to relate to symptoms of quitting smoking. But there is no one sentence that ties these details together.

4. **People have different tastes, but it seems that everyone loves movies.** The other sentences support the main idea found in this topic sentence and do not tell what the paragraph is mostly about.

Lesson 7

Page 54

If you like nightlife, there are plenty of clubs and restaurants.

Page 55

1. There are many ways to cook vegetables.

2. Possible answers include sentences 2–5 in the paragraph.

3. There are two sentences that add information: Steamed, baked, and grilled vegetables keep more of their vitamins than boiled vegetables. Fried vegetables keep their vitamins, too, but they are high in fat.

Page 56

1. Putting an ad in the personals column of a newspaper can be an easy and safe way to meet interesting people.

2. **(4) both 1 and 2** The paragraph says that personal ads are safe and easy but does not tell how to answer them.

3. **(3) your house or apartment** The paragraph says meeting at a coffee shop or other well-lighted public place is safe. The next sentence says that this person never has to know where you live. This implies that your home would not be a good place to meet someone for the first time.

Page 57

4. **(1) the first sentence** This is the only sentence that states the topic of the paragraph. It tells what the paragraph is mostly about. The other sentences are details that support the main idea.

5. **(2) small amounts of money.** This answer is found in the first sentence of the paragraph.

6. **(4) In most states, the fees for filing a claim are small, and you don't even need a lawyer.** This answer is found in the last sentence of the paragraph.

GED Skill Strategy, *pages 58–59*

Page 58

1. Getting healthy is a great goal for all of us.

2. The key to moving into a new home is good organization.

3. Weather forecasting is not an exact science.

4. **(b) There are three types of volcanoes.** The paragraph presents three types of volcanoes. Based on the passage, Choice (a) is not true.

5. **(a) The crowd loved Dani's performance.** The crowd roared with laughter. They enjoyed Dani's performance. Dani did not upset or shock the audience, so Choice (b) is incorrect.

GED Test-Taking Strategy

Page 61

1. **(2) help with cleanliness, protection, and hunting** When you thought about the purpose question, you looked for things that showed friendship between dogs and people. Choices (1) and (4) are the opposite of what was presented in the paragraph. Choice (3) was not in the paragraph at all.

2. **(4) They stand for the original thirteen colonies.** When you thought about the purpose question, you noticed the final decision. It tells how the stripes on the flag will be used. Choices (1) and (3) tell about earlier ways that the stripes were used on the flag. Choice (2) is not supported by the passage.

GED Test Practice, *pages 62–64*

Page 62

1. **(2) Hand washing helps prevent the spread of germs.** Choices (1), (3), and (4) do not tell what the paragraph is mainly about. They are details that support the main idea expressed in Choice (2).

2. **(2) You may spread your germs to others.** Choices (1), (3), and (4) are not supported by the details in the passage

3. **(3) Wash your hands.** The answer to the question is found in the fourth sentence of the paragraph. Choices (1), (2), and (4) do not tell what someone should do after rubbing their eyes.

Page 63

4. **(1) *The Old Farmer's Almanac* offers information, predictions, and advice.** This is the main idea that is implied by the information in the paragraph. Choices (2) and (3) are supporting details, but they are not the main point of the paragraph. Choice (4) is not in the paragraph at all.

5. **(4) all of the above** Choices (1), (2), and (3) are all supporting details that tell more about the main idea.

6. **(4) the year's phases of the moon** Choice (4) is correct because this is mentioned as something that you will find in *The Old Farmer's Almanac*. Choices (1) and (3) are not mentioned in the paragraph. Choice (2) is incorrect because the almanac has weather predictions, not exact weather conditions for specific days.

Page 64

7. **(3) It's easy to sign up for a class at the Art Center.** This is the topic sentence that tells what the paragraph is mostly about. Choices (1), (2), and (4) are supporting details.

8. (4) Send your form and payment to the address in the catalog. Choices (1), (2), and (3) all tell things you should do before you send the form and your payment to the address in the catalog.

Unit 3 Lesson 8

Page 66

1. (2) 3. (4)
2. (3) 4. (5)

Page 67

1. First 3. After that
2. Second 4. Finally

Page 68

1. You may have chosen three of the following words and phrases that show time order: 1943, The next day, A few days later, Then, Thirty minutes later, soon, Today

2. A farmer noticed that a small hill had grown in his cornfield.

3. There was an explosion.

Page 69

4. **(2) It tells about city growth over a period of years.** Choices (1) and (4) tell about different details in the passage, but not time order. Choice (3) is not correct because the paragraphs do not tell about life in U.S. cities.

5. **(4) About eight out of ten people lived in or near a city.** Choices (1), (2), and (3) are facts, but none of them give recent information.

6. **(3) 1916** Choices (1), (2), and (4) do not tell when almost half of the people in the United States lived in cities.

Lesson 9

Page 71

Words that compare
alike
both

Words that contrast
different
However
On the other hand
less

Page 72

1. **(1) how the lives of Lincoln and Kennedy were alike.** Choice (2) is incorrect because the paragraph is about how the two men were alike, not different. Choices (3) and (4) are incorrect because the paragraph contains facts about both Lincoln and Kennedy.

2. The lives of two famous presidents were strangely alike in many ways.

3. *alike, also, both, same*

Page 73

4. **(1) the first sentence** Choice (1) is correct because the first sentence contains the word *different*. Choices (2), (3), and (4) also contain clue words, but they do not give you the *first* clue that two things are being contrasted.

5. **(4) different** Choices (1), (2), and (3) are incorrect because these words and phrases are not found in the first sentence.

6. **(4) the kinds of food babies and adults need** The paragraph is mostly about how the food babies need is different from the food adults need. Choices (1), (2), and (3) tell about things that are not described in the paragraph.

Lesson 10

Page 74

Any one of the following is correct:

The earth shifts and moves.

Shock waves travel in many directions.

Buildings shake.

Streets crack.

The clue circled in the paragraph at the bottom of the page should be *As a result*.

Page 75

1. *when, cause*

2. Southern California had an air pollution problem for many years.

3. Scientists decided that cars were the biggest cause of ozone smog.

4. The plan has helped.

Page 76

1. **(4) all of the above** Choices (1), (2), and (3) are all correct.

2. **(3) As a result** Choices (1) and (2) are clue words, but they do not appear in the paragraph. Choice (4) is incorrect because both (1) and (2) are incorrect.

3. **(2) when people pat and speak to their pets** Choices (1) and (3) are incorrect because these are not causes for blood pressure dropping. Choice (4) is incorrect because choice (1) is wrong.

Page 77

4. **(1) The aloe plant can help treat burns.** All of the other choices are true, but they are details that support the main idea stated in choice (1).

5. **(3) The pain will lessen or stop almost immediately.** Choice (1) is incorrect because the leaf has to be broken to get the gel. Choice (2) is not mentioned in the paragraph. Choice (4) is not correct because both (1) and (2) are incorrect.

6. **(4) both (1) and (3).** *If* and *as a result* are clues for cause and effect found in the paragraph. Choice (2) is not a clue for cause and effect.

Lesson 11

Page 78

Topic sentence: Some home remedies tell you to do the opposite of what doctors would tell you to do.

The next three sentences make up the example.

Topic sentence: Although this type of suit can be hard to prove, many people have taken their cases to court and won.

The other sentences make up the example.

Page 79

1. Sentence (1): When you get a sprain, there are certain things you can do.

2. *first, then, finally*

3. Sentences (3) and (4).

4. **(4) examples** The main idea is that at one time Route 66 was considered one of the most interesting and exciting routes to travel. The writer includes two things that were of interest to travelers—seeing the world's largest prairie dog and having lunch in a hat-shaped restaurant. Choices (1), (2), and (3) do not correctly tell how the paragraph is organized.

Page 80

1. **(1) the Venus' flytrap is a carnivorous plant.** The information in choices (2), (3), and (4) is not mentioned.

2. **(3) The details explain how the Venus' flytrap catches an insect.** Choice (1) is not mentioned. Choices (2) and (4) are details from the story but do not give an example of how the plant is carnivorous.

3. **(4) both (1) and (2)** The growth of the population is shown as years pass. This is time order. The paragraph also contrasts the differences in population at different times. Choice (3) is incorrect because there are no examples of cause and effect in the paragraph.

Page 81

3. **(4) to make a comparison and show examples** Choice (1) is incorrect because there is no cause and effect in the paragraph. The sentences that follow *weather* and *climate* each give examples that support the main idea. Choices (2) and (3) are incorrect because they list only one of the two ways the paragraph is organized.

4. **(4) all of the above** The words in Choices (1), (2), and (3) are all clues for comparing, contrasting, or giving an example.

GED Skill Strategy, *pages 82–83*

Page 82

Circle years: 1783, 1799, 1848, and 1884
Underline clue words: *first, before, then* and *finally.*

The timeline should be similar to the one below.

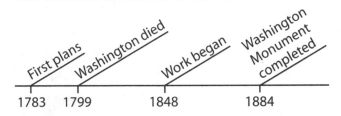

Page 83

Underline words that mean the same: *too, both.* Circle words that mean different: *but, on the other hand.*

GED Test-Taking Strategy

Page 85

1. Sample retellings of the main idea: Scientists didn't want the chicks to be friends with humans. Scientists did not want the chicks to need humans.

2. **(2) Ninety-nine California condors live in the wild. Others live in programs that will take care of them until they are freed.** Choices (1), (3), and (4) retell the important details from the first two paragraphs. Choice (2) is the best retelling of the main point of the last paragraph.

Page 86

1. **(4) Both have water slides and an arcade area.** Choices (1), (2), and (3) tell about differences between the two parks.

2. **(4) all of the above** Choices (1), (2) and (3) are all clues that tell you two things are being compared and contrasted.

3. **(2) River Park will be updated.** Choices (1), (3), and (4) are not mentioned.

Page 87

4. **(3) by giving steps that you should follow** The paragraph is organized to guide the reader step by step to take up a new sport. Choices (1) and (4) do not present the main organization of the paragraph. Choice (2) is incorrect because nothing is compared or contrasted.

5. **(4) time order** The words *First, Next,* and *Finally* are clues about how the paragraph is organized. Choice (1) is incorrect because the paragraph does not compare and contrast. Choice (2) is incorrect because the paragraph does not include examples of cause and effect. Choice (3) is incorrect because the paragraph does not give any examples.

6. **(3) Your physical problems might get worse.** For Choices (1) and (2), the subjects are talked about in the paragraph, but not in regard to health. Choice (4) is not mentioned in the paragraph.

Page 88

7. **(1) by telling a story about how Daniel fell in love** The main idea is Daniel Boone was devoted to his wife. The story is an example that shows the beginning of Daniel's devotion to his wife.

Choice (2) is incorrect because the effects of Daniel falling in love are not mentioned in the paragraph. Choice (3) is incorrect because Daniel is not compared before and after falling in love. Choice (4) is incorrect because no steps are given that show how Daniel fell in love.

8. **(1) One is about how Daniel Boone met his wife, Rebecca.** This sentence lets you know that the story about Daniel Boone meeting his wife is a folktale. "One" refers to "folktales" in the first sentence.

Unit 4 Lesson 12

Page 90

1. It is Terri's birthday.

2. Pat has made a cake with candles for Terri. Pat has also bought and wrapped presents for Terri. These are things you do for someone's birthday.

Page 91

1. The man is Mrs. Connelly's doctor.

2. The evidence that supports this inference is that the man is wearing a white coat. He takes Mrs. Connelly's pulse. He calls her by her formal name, and he asks how she is feeling.

3. The large ruby in Mrs. Connelly's ring, as well as having a doctor at her home, show that Mrs. Connelly is probably rich.

Page 92

1. a nurse

2. Jackie is a hard worker.

3. **(2) old.** You can infer that Tom is old because he has grey hair, needs reading glasses, walks with a cane, and has trouble getting out of a chair. Therefore, Choice (1) is incorrect. Choice (3) is incorrect

because the paragraph does not say or imply that Tom is either poor or rich. Choice (4) is incorrect because the paragraph describes Tom's physical problems.

4. **(3) has trouble walking.** Tom is older and the paragraph describes that he has trouble getting out of his chair. The paragraph also states that Tom uses a cane. It is logical to infer that Tom would have trouble walking Choices (1), (2), and (4) are not supported by the evidence.

Page 93

5. **(4) both (1) and (2)** Both Choices (1) and (2) are implied in the ad. Gas is mentioned in the ad, but it is described as something the car may use too much of. Brands are not mentioned. Therefore, Choice (3) is incorrect.

6. **(3) Grime Out takes very little time to work.** This inference makes sense because the ad says that "After using just one bottle" your car will run better. Choices (1), (2), and (4) give the opposite of the correct information.

Lesson 13

Page 95

1. The following are sample conclusions: Pluto is the ninth planet from the sun. It will be much colder than the temperature on Mars, which is around -191°F. Since Pluto is the farthest planet from the sun, it will have the coldest surface temperature.

2. Earth

Page 96

1. Sample conclusion: The Martins live by a strict schedule.

2. A time is given for each activity, and the Martins follow this pattern every day.

3. **(2) it's warm and pleasant in Florida.** Choices (1) and (3) are incorrect because they tell information that is the opposite of what is presented in the paragraph. Choice (4) tells information that is not mentioned and cannot be logically inferred.

Page 97

4. **(1) a balanced diet includes many different foods.** The first item in the list says that you should "eat a variety of foods." The third item gives examples of the foods you should eat. Choice (2) is incorrect because some fat is needed in the diet. Choice (3) is incorrect because although fruits and vegetables are important, they are not the only foods you should eat. Choice (4) is incorrect because it is not stated in the passage and can not be logically inferred.

5. **(2) you should eat more than one serving of many kinds of foods each day.** The third item in the bulleted list implies that this is true. Choice (1) is incorrect because item one in the list says to eat a variety of foods. Choices (3) and (4) are not stated or implied by the passage.

6. **(3) some foods are better for you than others.** Choice (1) is incorrect because it tells information that is the opposite of what is presented in the paragraph. Choices (2) and (4) are incorrect because this information is not stated nor can it be concluded from the information given.

Lesson 14

Page 99

There are no clue words in the first paragraph.

<u>I think</u> it's awful that I have to breathe smoke all day. <u>In my opinion</u>, smoking should be illegal in all public places.

1. **(b) the second paragraph** The second paragraph includes the clue words "I think" and "in my opinion." Not everyone would agree with what is stated in this paragraph.

2. **(a) the first paragraph** This paragraph gives three facts that can be checked.

Page 100

1. **(2) It's good but not southern.** Choice (1) is incorrect because the writer uses words like "tender and crisp" and "delicious." Choice (3) is incorrect because the writer has some doubts about the food. Choice (4) is incorrect because the writer does state his opinion.

2. **(4) The writer doesn't give an opinion.** The writer does not give any opinions in the article, only facts. Choices (1), (2), and (3) are incorrect because they are opinions.

Page 101

3. **(3) The writer wants a law that requires people to vote.** Choice (1) is incorrect because the paragraph does not tell how to get a passport. Choice (2) is incorrect because the writer does not talk about existing laws. Choice (4) is incorrect because the writer does not want to stop people from traveling outside the country.

4. **(1) Less than 55 percent of U.S. citizens vote in presidential elections.** Choice (2) is true, but it does not support the writer's opinion. Choice (3) is not true. Choice (4) is an opinion, not a fact.

5. **(4) both (1) and (2)** The phrases in Choice (1) and (2) are found in the paragraph. Choice (3) does indicate an opinion is being given, but this phrase is not found in the paragraph.

Lesson 15

Page 103

1. B
2. N
3. N
4. B

Page 104

There are several possible answers. The following is a sample response:

1. The writer thinks the head of the school board is a phony.

2. "Then he rolled up his shirtsleeves to look like a man of the people." This shows that the head of the school board is trying to appear as something that he really isn't. The writer doesn't think the head of the school board is "a man of the people."

3. The writer thinks that the head of the school board does not care about the people or their concerns. The writer says "He smiled as if he cared about the people in the room, but his eyes were cold." The writer thinks that the head of the school board is just pretending to care.

Page 105

4. **(3) One is biased against Kate Reeves, and one is not.** Choice (1) is incorrect because both are about the school and Ms. Reeves. Choice (2) is incorrect because the question asks how the articles are different, not how they are alike. Choice (4) is incorrect because both articles mention the lawsuit.

5. **(4) both (1) and (3)** Look back at the articles to see how the words are used. In article 2, you see that "gruff" (Choice 1) and "emotional" (Choice 3) are used to describe Ms. Reeves in an unfavorable way. "Suing" (Choice 2) is used in both articles to tell of a legal action. The word is not used to create a response in the reader.

6. **(4) She was a bad teacher who was treated fairly.** The writer of article 2 justifies her firing, blaming the teacher rather than students for their poor grades. Choice (1) is the opposite view of the view given in article 2. Choice (2) is not mentioned or implied in either article. However, article 1 does imply that Kate Reeves thinks that school policies regarding athletes are wrong. Choice (3) is not true, based on the articles. She refused to do what the university officials told her to do.

GED Skill Strategy, *pages 106–107*

Page 106

1. **(a) in the city**

2. There are sounds of buses and cars on the streets below the apartment. This is common in the city.

3. Sample responses:
The family is new to the United States. They are just getting started in this country. They do not have much money.

Page 107

1. believe

2. The writer wants me to feel that people who do not wear seat belts are poor drivers who should be punished.

3. careless

GED Test-Taking Strategy

Page 109

1. **(2) to provide faster mail service to California** Choice (1) is incorrect because California already had mail service—by stagecoach. Choice (3) is incorrect because the Midwest is not mentioned. Choice (4) is incorrect because that was not the goal of those who created the service.

2. **(3) people can be swept out to sea** Choice (1) is incorrect because a tsunami is the result of an earthquake, not the cause. Choices (2) and (4) are not mentioned in the paragraph.

Page 110

1. **(3) He paints people.** This inference is based on what Cobb is known for saying, "I paint them as I see them." The word *them* probably refers to the people he meets. Choices (1) and (2) are incorrect because this information is not given in the paragraph. Choice (4) is incorrect because his saying most likely refers to people, not buildings.

2. **(1) It will show a new way of looking at people's lives.** Because the program ends with a focus on his canvas, it will show the artist's own unique view. Choices (2), (3), and (4) are not supported.

3. **(2) Cobb never stays long in one community.** He is called a "wandering artist." Choice (1) is incorrect because Cobb will probably meet a variety of people to keep the program interesting. Choice (3) is incorrect because there is no indication that Cobb will marry. Choice (4) is incorrect because though Cobb seems matter-of-fact, he does not seem heartless.

Page 111

4. **(4) Manners are always changing.** The writer contrasts what was once acceptable with what is now acceptable. This shows that manners have changed. Choice (1) is an incorrect conclusion. The paragraph suggests that it is not polite for either sex to smoke in public. Choice (2) is incorrect because it says that an old rule is the correct rule for today. Choice (3) is incorrect because the paragraph mainly tells about manners and being polite.

5. **(1) believe** This word is a clue that an opinion will follow. Choices (2), (3), and (4) are not clue words that signal an opinion.

6. **(2) They selfishly grab the best for themselves.** The word *selfishly* is a loaded word that the writer uses to get the reader to feel the same way. Choices (1), (3), and (4) are statements from the passage that do not use emotional, or loaded, language.

Page 112

7. **(1) Drake's performance was "flawless."** Choice (2) also shows bias, but it is not about *The Great Jewel Caper.* Choices (3) and (4) are factual statements; they do not show bias or answer the question.

8. **(4) *The Great Jewel Caper* opens this weekend.** Choice (1) says that Drake was unforgettable, expressing an opinion. Choice (2) says that her performance was flawless, also an opinion. Choice (3) says that her last movie was powerful, which is also an opinion.

Unit 5 Lesson 16

Page 114

1. Aunt Tiger is stocky and round.

2. Aunt Tiger speaks her mind; she complains a lot.

Page 115

1. Seoul

2. They are standing on a snow-dusted hill outside the city wall.

Page 116

1. Lester

2. on a prairie

3. **(b)** She has a good sense of humor.

Page 117

4. **(3) She has ash-blonde hair and doesn't smile.** Choice (1) is incorrect because the passage doesn't mention the woman being tall, and the man is the one who is sunburned. Choice (2) is incorrect because the woman has ash-blonde hair, not brown. The color of her eyes is not mentioned. Choice (4) is incorrect because it is the man who folds his arms and has dull eyes.

5. **(1) He is not in a good mood.** The man looks sullen and sits with his arms folded. These details show that he is not in a good mood. Choices (2), (3) and (4) are incorrect because there are no details, stated or inferred, to support them.

Lesson 17

Page 118

Action 2 One man put a wrench on the hydrant, and two other men put a hose onto the tank.
Action 4 The man with the wrench opened the valve.

Page 119

1. Mark and the animal.

2. He swings himself up into a tree.

Page 120

1. He was happy and relieved.

2. There might have been a problem if Ben was not there to deliver the baby.

Page 121

3. **(2) T.J. has put soil on the roof, and the owner wants the soil off.** Choices (1) and (3) may be true statements, but neither one shows the conflict in the passage. Choice (4) is incorrect because the owner wants the soil off his roof.

4. **(4) T.J. argues with him.** Choices (1), (2), and (3) are all incorrect because there are no details in the story to support them. In the last line of the passage, T.J. is upset after the owner states that the soil is to be shoveled off tomorrow, and he tells the owner why he thinks it is unfair.

Lesson 18

Page 122

These sentences should be underlined: "But man is not made for defeat," and "A man can be destroyed but not defeated."

Page 123

1. a feeling of hope or peace

2. Possible answers: They heard and felt the breath of spring, and they stirred with new life and hope. There was a good, new smell in the air, a smell of earth waking after its long sleep.

Page 124

1. She thinks the pearl is evil.

2. He wants to keep the pearl so that they can afford to send their son to school.

3. Sample answer: Parents are willing to do anything for their children.

Page 125

4. **(2) an uneasy mood** The characters are watchful and careful. The setting is a deserted place. The dogs howl and scurry around. The characters may not be safe. Choice (1) is incorrect because the details in the passage do not support any spiritual ideas. Choice (3) is incorrect because the feeling of the passage is dark, not adventurous. Choice (4) is incorrect because the main characters do not appear to be angry. They appear to be quiet and watchful, helping to create the uneasy mood.

5. **(4) The huts looked like ghosts in the cold light.** This answer suggests something strange, helping to create the uneasy mood. The details in Choices (1), (2) and (3) do not help create this mood.

Lesson 19

Page 126

The words that rhyme in stanza 1 are *inside* and *dried*.

The words that rhyme in stanza 2 are *find* and *mind*.

There are two stanzas in the poem.

Page 127

Possible answers:

1. a bright red rose—sight

2. thick, sweet cream—sight, touch, taste

3. a bird's cheerful song—sound

4. the sun and a lamp

5. a bee sting and a fire

Page 128

1. **(3) water** Choice (1) is incorrect because that is what the world is compared to in the fifth line of the poem. Choices (2) and (4) are incorrect because the night and a plain are not being compared to anything in the poem.

2. **(2) Have seen the world awaken like a child** The way that the world awakens and the way a child awakens are compared. Choices (1) and (3) do not represent comparisons. Choice (1) tells of a series of actions. Choice (3) is a statement of what the narrator has seen. Choice (4) is not correct because Choice (1) is incorrect.

3. **(3) It is a hopeful time of day.** Choices (1) and (2) are incorrect because they are not supported by the details in the poem, or the mood of the poem. Choice (4) is incorrect because the poem does not say anything about a child's favorite time of day. The poem only states that it is dawn.

Page 129

4. **(2) a broken-winged bird** When the poet uses the words "Life is . . ." he begins a comparison between life and something else—in this case, "a broken-winged bird." Choices (1), (3), and (4) are incorrect because life is not compared to these.

5. **(3) a barren field** Again, the poet uses the words "Life is . . ." to begin a comparison. In this case, life is compared to a barren field. Choices (1), (2), and (4) are incorrect because these are not compared to life in the poem.

6. **(4) sight and touch** The words create imagery that helps the reader "see" the field (sight) with the word *barren* and "feel" how cold it is with the word *frozen* (touch). Choice (1) is incorrect because the imagery does not appeal to the sense of taste. Choices (2) and (3) are incorrect because the imagery does not appeal to the sense of hearing.

GED Skill Strategy, *pages 130–131*

Page 130

Exercise 1

1. Kate
2. Kate and Seth talk about sore joints and grandchildren.
3. She is pacing as she thinks about visiting Seth's house.

Page 131

Exercise 2

1. in the backyard at Seth's house
2. The sun is setting, so you can tell that it is early evening.
3. Kate arrives at Seth's house and is taken into the backyard. There, Seth greets her and introduces her to his daughter and grandson.

GED Test-Taking Strategy

Page 133

1. **(4) the road** Choice (1) is incorrect because the sea in the poem does not describe a real sea; it is a comparison to describe the road or asphalt. Choice (2) is incorrect because the words *auto* and *mobile* are found in lines 11 and 12. Choice (3) is incorrect because the narrator is on a skateboard, skimming the asphalt sea.

2. **(1) a sailor** The line in the poem says, "I'm the sailor . . ." Choices (2), (3), and (4) are mentioned in the poem, but are not mentioned in line 6.

GED Test Practice, *pages 134–136*

Page 134

1. **(3) food and shelter** The soldier states this when the main character asks what he wants. While the soldier might benefit from Choices (1), (2), and (4), he does not ask for these things.

2. **(4) young and bearded** There are other possible words to describe the character, but Choices (1), (2) and (3) all have one incorrect or unsupported answer in the pairs provided.

Page 135

3. **(4) The only sound was the clear, lonely song of a spring bird.** Choices (1), (2), and (3) are incorrect because the second sentence of the paragraph mentions what time of year the events take place. None of the other answer choices suggest any information about the setting.

4. **(4) just before dawn** Choices (1), (2), and (3) are incorrect because the second sentence of the paragraph mentions the "darkness outside." Later the passage states that the doctor's "nightshirt" was slipping over his shoulder. From this, you can conclude that it is most likely just before dawn.

5. **(4) tense** "Tenseness" is the word used by the author to describe the feeling in the room at both the beginning and end of the paragraph. Choices (1), (2) and (3) are not correct because none of these feelings are supported by the details in the paragraph.

Page 136

6. **(2) touch and taste** The first verse is about how the peach feels. The second verse is about how the peach tastes. Choices (1), (3), and (4) are incorrect because there is no imagery that helps the reader hear how the peach sounds, see how the peach looks, or sense what the peach smells like.

Reading Posttest, *pages 137–144*

Page 137

1. **(1) setting a timer** Since the first two sentences of the paragraph focus on an oven timer, you can predict that the rest of the paragraph will be about how to set the timer. Choices (2), (3), and (4) are all mentioned, but they only offer supporting information about how to set the timer.

2. **(2) Set the start dial for the time that the oven should turn on.** This step is given before the step on how to set the stop time. Choice (1) is incorrect because checking that the oven is set to the correct temperature is the last step. Choice (3) is incorrect because the control knob should be set to "Timed Bake," not to "Off." Choice (4) is incorrect because the main clock should show the current time of day, not the start time.

Page 139

3. **(4) They had to fight to improve things for everyone.** Choices (1), (2), and (3) are not supported by the poem.

4. **(3) sound.** Choices (1), (2), and (4) are incorrect because there is nothing in these lines that appeal to the senses of smell, touch, or taste, only sound.

5. **(1) make someone appear guilty.** This definition is given in the rest of the sentence following the word *incriminate*. Choice (2) tells about a different right. Choice (3) is an action taken by police. Choice (4) is not the meaning given in the paragraph for *incriminate*.

6. **(2) After a person is read his or her rights, anything he or she says can be used as evidence in court.** Choice (1) is incorrect because the passage is about the rights that people have after they are arrested. Choice (3) is incorrect because there is nothing in the paragraph that states or suggests that most people who are arrested remain silent. Choice (4) is incorrect because asking for a lawyer does not incriminate you.

Page 140

7. **(1) There are some easy ways to get people to start talking to you.** This answer is stated in the third sentence of the paragraph. The other information in the paragraph supports this idea. Choices (2), (3), and (4) are in the paragraph but are less important ideas.

8. **(1) a T-shirt with a funny saying** This is specifically mentioned in the passage. Choices (2), (3), and (4) are not mentioned in the paragraph.

9. **(4) wear something unusual.** This example is given in the paragraph as one thing you can do to make people talk to you. Choice (1) is the opposite of the advice given in the paragraph. Choice (2) is described as something that is difficult to do. Choice (3) is not mentioned.

Page 141

10. **(1) cares about other people's feelings.** This definition is suggested in the third sentence, after the word *considerate* appears. Choice (2) gives the opposite definition. Choices (3) and (4) are incorrect because these definitions are not given or suggested in the paragraph.

11. **(4) Nonsmokers scream about their "right" to breathe clean air.** The loaded word *scream* and the use of quotation marks with the word *right* show how the writer feels about nonsmokers and their complaints. Choices (1), (2), and (3) all give ideas that do not show any bias.

12. **(3) I believe that smokers have rights, too!** The phrase "I believe" shows that the writer of the letter is expressing an opinion. Choices (1), (2), and (4) all present facts.

Page 142

13. **(2) working hours and overtime pay options** The work rules describe a typical workweek and the overtime pay options for employees who work more than 40 hours per week. Choices (1) and (4) are not correct because they only state one idea in the memo, not what the memo is mainly about. Choice (3) is incorrect because the duties of managers are not described.

14. **(2) overtime pay.** This is stated in the memo. Choices (1), (3), and (4) are not related to working more than forty hours.

15. **(1) job loss** This is stated in the first section of the memo. Choices (2), (3), and (4) are not related to failure to answer an emergency call.

Page 143

16. **(1) put money into a bank.** Choices (2), (3), and (4) are all meanings for the word *deposit*, but these meanings do not apply to the way that the word is used in the passage.

17. **(1) The amount of interest charged for a loan is higher.** This answer can be figured out from the last sentence in the passage. Choices (2), (3), and (4) are incorrect.

Page 144

18. **(4) is in a hospital.** Information about bandages suggest that the narrator is in a hospital. Choices (1), (2), and (3) give information that is different from what is described in the passage.

19. **(1) He was injured in a battle.** Choices (2), (3), and (4) give information that is not stated or supported by the paragraph.

20. **(2) during the day** The first and last sentences mention bright sunlight. Choices (1), (3), and (4) are all times when there is no sunlight or when the sun is no longer very bright.